COCK AND
BULL STORIES

A RANDOM HOUSE BOOK published by Random House New Zealand
18 Poland Road, Glenfield, Auckland, New Zealand

For more information about our titles go to www.randomhouse.co.nz

A catalogue record for this book is available from the National Library of New Zealand

Random House New Zealand is part of the Random House Group
New York   London   Sydney   Auckland   Delhi   Johannesburg

First published 2011. Reprinted 2011.

© 2011 Peter Anderson and Peter Jerram; illustrations by Ashley Smith

The moral rights of the author have been asserted

ISBN 978 1 86979 519 1

This book is copyright. Except for the purposes of fair reviewing no part of this publication may be reproduced or transmitted in any form or by any means, electronic or mechanical, including photocopying, recording or any information storage and retrieval system, without permission in writing from the publisher.

Design: Megan van Staden
Cover illustration: Ashley Smith
Printed in New Zealand by Printlink

COCK AND BULL STORIES

Tales from Two Kiwi Country Vets

RANDOM HOUSE
NEW ZEALAND

Peter Jerram & Peter Anderson

*To our wives Ally and Chick who, through all
the ups and downs, made it possible*

CONTENTS

Foreword	9
In The Beginning — PJ	13
Early Days — PA	17
After-hours Ripper — PJ	27
Wake-up Calls — PA	31
Molesworth — PJ	39
The Worst Day of My Career — PA	45
Pachyderms and Potatoes — PJ	53
Race Day — PA	57
Pony Club Anecdotes — PJ	63
Cock and Bull Story — PA	69
Nautical Matters — PJ	75
Mr Scrope and Toby — PA	89
Debt Collection — PJ	93
Flying and Work — PA	97
The Galloping Major — PJ	111
Driving to the Job — PA	115
Flannelled Oafs — PJ	123
Alternative Medicines — PA	131
Deer Things — PJ	135
Roo — PA	143
Faecal Facials — PJ	149

Dropping Bulls — PA	**153**
Trusting Friendships — PJ	**159**
Flying and Passengers — PA	**163**
Punctuality — PJ	**171**
At the Zoo — PA	**175**
The Two Ronnies — PJ	**183**
The Other Side — PJ	**191**
A Stint in Kosovo — PA	**195**
The Wall of Death — PJ	**205**
Ima Dreamer — PA	**209**
Gymnastics and Testicles — PJ	**217**
Deer Capture Days — PA	**223**
Of Roofs and Fingers — PJ	**231**
Fainters — PA	**235**
Traffic Cops — PJ	**241**
Hospital Visits — PA	**247**
Dogs Who Will Always Love Me — PJ	**255**
Large Animal Practice — PA	**263**
All at Sea — PJ	**269**
Reflections — PA	**275**
Darkness and Light — PJ	**283**

FOREWORD

Two recurrent themes ebb and flow throughout this highly engaging and informative book — a sense of fun and a sense of dedication. Those themes will be recognised by many in the Marlborough community who have dealt with Peter Anderson and Peter Jerram over some 35 years, and carry into print the very attributes displayed by these larger-than-life characters in their veterinary practice.

These two blokes have successfully struck a balance, both in life and now in print, between these attributes. One is the mix of knowledge, skills, empathy and sensitivity required to successfully operate as dedicated vets servicing both small and large animal veterinary needs. The other is what one passage describes as a 'larrikin' approach to life.

The outcome is a series of anecdotes that inform and delight. They also convey realistically, and often highly amusingly, the colour and feel of the Marlborough countryside and the people who make a living within it.

The emphasis on sheep and beef farming practices and their

associated humour will strike a ready chord with the farming community and those who service that community in provincial towns. But the appeal of this book is broader than that. The humour and the insights into country life will equally intrigue and amuse a wider audience in the cities.

The focus is naturally on Marlborough's dry country, encompassing major valleys and rugged mountain ranges, and the influence of the Marlborough Sounds complex. The authors' travel antics and experiences have arisen from the challenge of servicing a far-flung clientele across a large and geographically challenging province. To many, the descriptions of the reliance of the 'flying vet' Pete Anderson on a variety of aeroplanes, and his mix of good luck as well as good management in surviving a series of close calls, will add a uniqueness to this book not encountered in any other.

But the book also ranges far beyond those Marlborough settings. Intriguing chapters describe a voyage on a vessel carrying some 100,000 sheep to Saudi Arabia, and an extended advisory stay in war-torn Kosovo.

I highly commend this book to anyone keen to catch a glimpse of veterinary life in a New Zealand provincial setting, while at the same time enjoying the humour and warmth that life naturally provides.

In short it is a cracker.

Ron Crosby
Blenheim
April 2011

IN THE BEGINNING — PJ

I'll never forget the day I first met the man. I had walked into the Graham Veterinary Club on a Monday morning. It was 1978 and the appraising but friendly eyes looked at me in penetrating fashion.

'Hello,' I said, 'I'm Peter Jerram.'

'Gidday. Pete Anderson.' The expression relaxed and a grin spread across that friendly bear-like face. By the end of the day we'd laughed at several things, mostly smutty, and at the end of a week we were friends.

I was a student then, with a year to go at vet school. Pete had worked in Blenheim for three years. We were similar ages, but I'd stuffed around for a few more years than he had, and we had a lot in common.

Thirty-one years later, as I write this, we're still good friends. We know each others' families almost as our own. We've shared fun, pain, triumph and disaster. We've had a financial roller coaster, usually on the lower part of the sine wave, and occasional successes. I've visited him in hospital on at least eight occasions that I can think of (and once even took an Elizabethan collar in

— so he couldn't lick out his sutures — when he'd had his piles operated on; at least the nurses thought it was funny). We've holidayed together, camped, tramped, hunted, fished and sailed together. We've socialised together, and still do, though never in each other's faces.

I've been privileged enough to speak for Pete at his father Derek's funeral after that lovely man and Pete's mother, knowing Derek was dying, had instructed Pete before he left not to interrupt a major European holiday.

Peter Anderson (PA) is a legendary sheep veterinarian, who developed into a primary consulting veterinarian, but many will not know he was a very fine small animal soft tissue surgeon for several years. He's a lovely warm man, as all who know him will agree. And I have been extremely fortunate to work with him. I was philosophically a sheep farmer's vet also, and that was a primary bond between us.

About 10 years after we'd been in business together we realised that we weren't running it as a business. In the typical style of professionals of that era, we knew nothing of business principles, nothing of marketing, and computers barely existed. The monthly accounts were shambolic. We employed a facilitator, a business management veterinarian, to look at our business with us. John O'Flaherty helped us identify the need for someone to stay in the clinic and run the business. That person would therefore do the bulk of the small animal work and the other partner would do the large animal work. I realised right then that my life was changing forever. Small animals was never my first choice as a vet, but I was interested in learning about the business, and being in charge of the farm animal health sales, and Pete was very happy to let that be, while indulging in his flying at the same time.

So apart from some sheep AI (artificial insemination) with the laparoscope, and a few after-hours calls, I became a small animal vet — mostly just a competent one, I think — and I had a large input into the business management. But I've always missed the farm work, and in particular the contact with sheep and beef farmers, that wonderful group of men and women who have formed the heart and soul of New Zealand for several generations. Because I spent nearly three years of my young life working on sheep and beef farms and runs in the South Island high country, I've always had a soft spot for that part of our land and the people who farm it. In the last few years dairying has multiplied at an amazing, and more than slightly disturbing rate, and sheep farmers are becoming somewhat less of a force economically, but my heart still lies with them. (The expansion of dairying is disturbing, because of the nature of the new, huge dairy farms, really giant farming factories, and the intensity of their production systems. There are animal health and animal welfare issues inherent in systems where individual cows get little attention and have chronically low body condition scores; there are environmental issues in water quality, water quantity, and aquifer nitrification.)

So back to Pete's and my professional relationship: at that stage our two paths began to diverge.

A lot of the stories in this book are from the earlier times when we were young, pretty uninhibited, and shared mostly farmer experiences. We saw humour in most situations, and with gathering age one wonders why that quality diminishes. But despite the divergence, and some differences in the direction of the business, the friendship has remained. It has been my very great fortune to have had a business partner who I respect hugely for his achievements, who I love like a brother.

Four years into a relatively early retirement, a bit worn out by nearly 30 years on the front lines, as it were, I look forward to many more good times with the Andersons. This book is a small, mostly non-sequential and fleeting look at some of the things which amused us. We hope they do the same for you.

At some early stage in our partnership as Anderson and Jerram Veterinary Clinic, we fell prey to a salesman (or -woman, probably the latter where Anderson was concerned) who convinced us that a ballpoint pen with our clinic name on it would be good for business. We chose the biggest they had — large triangular pens. We shamelessly stole the cartoon figures of Dog and Cecil the Ram, famous Murray Ball *Footrot Flats* characters. (Murray if you ever read this, which I doubt, would a couple of bottles of Sauvignon be OK?) We had one animal character at each end of the pen and the caption read 'I Got Nicked at Pete and Pete's Pussy Parlour'. Where the name came from, the memory fails, but it stuck, and those pens were around for years.

When we came to put this book together, 'Pete and Pete's Pussy Parlour' seemed just the right title. Our publisher, sadly, didn't agree and our wives were a bit dubious too, so we reluctantly let that name slip. The stories in this book have been slightly sanitised, but it is about the earlier period of our career together when we could get away with being larrikins. And just occasionally we still try.

EARLY DAYS — PA

A vet student walked into the clinic one morning and influenced my life forever. Peter Jerram had arrived to spend some time with us at the Graham Veterinary Club in Blenheim. It all came about after I had been talking to a classmate who mentioned that a good friend of his who had been at Lincoln University with him in a previous life was looking for somewhere to do some 'prac' work. Would it be OK if he came to us? 'Prac' work is what vet students do to gain some experience in veterinary practice before they graduate.

'He's a bit like you and me, Pete,' Bruce Taylor explained. 'He's also done another degree, got a bit bored with his job, and then decided to do the vet degree. Now he's in his final year. You'll like him. He's a hard case and a good bugger.'

Well I'm not too sure that PJ gained much useful experience from me but we hit it off immediately. He *was* a good bugger. While doing his 'prac' work he stayed with my wife Chick and me. It was hard not to like this mature (he is a year older than me) final year vet student with the twinkling eyes and ready laugh.

He was exceptionally quick witted and had a delightful sense of humour. We seemed to enjoy similar things and to have similar interests. We soon became good friends.

So why and how did our partnership start the way it did? Well, chance and good luck and making good decisions all played their part. Shortly before graduating with my veterinary degree from Massey University in Palmerston North, I had the good fortune to be offered a job at the Graham Veterinary Club in Blenheim. By chance I had heard one day towards the end of my final year that two local Vet Club directors were in Palmerston North. I made myself known to them and I guess I must have got on well with them. Later I got a job interview and then in the middle of final exams heard I had been accepted. Jobs were not easy to come by at that time so you tended to take what you could get. So after graduating, Chick, whom I had married a couple of years earlier, and I moved to Blenheim. Marlborough would be great for two or three years, then we would get a bit of overseas experience, return to New Zealand somewhere and settle down — well, that was the plan.

If we had had the choice we certainly wouldn't have chosen Blenheim. My earlier impressions were not that favourable. All my experiences with the place were associated with hitchhiking to catch the interisland ferry to or from Massey and home, in the Hundalees, south of Kaikoura. I had never found the place easy to hitch out of, although the image I presented probably didn't help — often bearded, sometimes with longish hair, filthy duffel coat, battered pack, and really pretty scruffy. No doubt I smelt as bad as I looked. I got to know a few of the culverts between Blenheim and Seddon, a village south of Blenheim, which while uncomfortable did keep one dry at night.

Despite my initial reservations, though, it didn't take long after arriving in Marlborough to realise the place was all we wanted. Over 35 years later we are still here! At the time the exciting emerging wine and mussel industries and a fairly buoyant farming community were driving the local economy. For my part I had the ability to fish in some of the district's idyllic rivers and in the Marlborough Sounds and the East Coast. I quickly learnt to dive and I had the chance to finally learn to fly. Flying had been a life-time dream and getting my pilot's licence was a promise I had made myself if I ever graduated. Meanwhile Chick pursued her passion for horse riding.

I was also blessed with having two more experienced and great vets to work with and learn from, Alan Stockley and Henk Brethouer. And finally but most importantly the clients, especially the rural ones, were a delight to work for and many were quickly becoming good friends.

However, nothing lasts, and within two years Henk returned with his family to Holland. Apart from David Sim, a very able horse vet who had just set up in the area, Alan and I were for a while the only vets in the northeast corner of the South Island, covering the Marlborough Sounds in the north, to Nelson Lakes and Rai Valley in the west, and as far south as Hanmer Springs. For a while we also had to cover for Kaikoura when they were without a vet.

After Henk and, shortly afterwards, Alan left, a few vets came and went but none lasted too long in Marlborough. What discouraged most from staying was the amount of driving they had to do to get to the farms. A full day might involve only a couple of calls but at least five hours' driving, mostly on narrow, dusty gravel roads. Many roads are still unsealed in the area but at least we now have comfortable, air-conditioned cars.

Anyway, around the time I first met PJ, Chick's and my lives were entering another era with the arrival of our first child, Caroline. Any thought of getting some overseas experience were now put on the back burner. We would have to stay a while. It was now the late 1970s and we were becoming very busy with an increased dairy and sheep and beef workload as well as an expanding small animal clientele. Blenheim was growing. So we were on the lookout for another vet to join the team of three youngish vets. I hoped PJ might be interested in being that person when he graduated at the end of the year. He was keen, and it wasn't hard to convince the committee of the Graham Veterinary Club that Pete would make a great fourth vet. So shortly after he graduated, he and Ally and their young son, Tom, arrived in Blenheim.

Pete's ability to make the best of any situation, to grab any opportunity, and to enjoy what Marlborough had to offer meant he very soon settled into the area. It didn't take long before he and I developed a healthy working and social relationship. We respected each other's strengths and weaknesses and utilised that knowledge in the best way possible. Together we planned how to improve the services the club provided, to get into farmer education and have workshops on animal health issues and to keep 'upskilling'. We like to think we did, but working in a 'Club' environment where one is an employee and on a set salary, a lack of return for extra input soon dampens any enthusiasm for progress.

So three years later PJ, Ally, Chick and I set up shop down the road and took Jill, one of the nurses, with us. As to be expected it was not a popular move with the club committee, but at least a couple of them acknowledged and accepted our decision with good grace and we will always appreciate their attitude. Neither family, both with young children now, had any cash, so we borrowed and leased everything. In fact Ally gave birth to their third child, Pip, the day we opened as 'Pete and Pete's Pussy Parlour'. Having two Petes could create confusion at times, including in this book, so we became known as PA and PJ. Once, a very attractive German vet student doing work experience with us decided that as she couldn't remember who was who and PJ was a little lighter, he would become Pete-Thin and I would be Pete-Thick. However, in the book we refer to each other by our initials — I prefer that!

In the early days cheap secondhand Datsun Sunny station wagons that bounced and blew all over the road kept us mobile for a couple of years, an old house was knocked into a sort of vet clinic shape over a couple of weekends, and basic surgical equipment was leased from an understanding insurance company. However, it did include the best X-ray machine and the best anaesthetic machine we could get our hands on. We could get by with secondhand cars and a cramped building but we were not prepared to compromise our skills and expertise with second-rate diagnostic and surgical equipment.

We survived more by good fortune than good management. The share market was in its boom days and there seemed to be money around. However, our accountant warned us that really things were not looking too good. We appreciated we were not that efficient, both of us trying to be everything to everyone, and both of us sometimes taking responsibility for everything, and at other times neither of us for anything. We bounced from day to day and then shared the after-hours and weekend duties. We worked long hours right at the time when we should have been spending more time with our young families. We were not often there to help our long-suffering and understanding wives, who were also working in the business, looking after the books and on many days manning the office and being receptionist and cleaner. Ally was also teaching while Chick had various other part-time jobs and eventually developed a very successful catering business.

The turning point came after a weekend retreat with a facilitator who helped us significantly and gave us some direction. A business plan (what the hell was one of those?) was written and responsibilities for different areas of the business were established. The need for staff changes was obvious: we needed another assistant/receptionist and we needed another vet. Despite the downturn in the economy and the share market crash and businesses elsewhere retrenching, we were going to expand. We employed a lovely and brilliant new graduate, Mandy Batchelor, and we shifted to bigger premises. We were on the move again.

Throughout our partnership PJ and I have always strived to improve our knowledge and expertise in the areas we enjoyed the most and were best at. While we both enjoyed the small animal work, with production animals we both also had a preference for sheep and beef cattle. Dairy cows were not our favourite species. Eventually I became the large animal (LA) vet and Pete concentrated more on small animal (SA) work and the technically demanding and intricate work, and business management. His business acumen was far more likely to benefit the practice than mine. I also had the ability to fly to many of the LA jobs, which saved a significant amount of time.

While we could have both gone either way, once the decision was made that I would manage the large and production animal side of the business and PJ would look after the domestic animals and retail side, it was amazing how quickly I found it difficult to go back and work confidently in the clinic. I would sometimes feel (fleetingly) sorry for PJ when I was enjoying a beautiful day out, working in good company and not being stressed by the day-to-day hassles more often experienced in small animal practice. On the other hand I occasionally envied him, especially when working long days in wet, cold weather well into the night, miles from home.

PJ became a very competent and popular small animal vet and developed his orthopaedic skills to a high degree, a definite requirement in a rural environment with many working dogs. However, his real claim to fame would be his skill as a dog reproductive expert. By the time he retired he was one of the country's leading experts on reproductive problems in bitches, collecting and using frozen dog semen. This did not come without cost and required several trips to overseas conferences and to study alongside the world's best. The development of expertise alongside natural ability requires study, time and money, a fact that many clients who go for the cheap option often fail to appreciate. He also became extremely competent at sheep artificial insemination (AI) and together we were among the first to get into embryo transfer in sheep, goats, and deer.

Although I have always enjoyed working with small animals and most of their owners, the veterinary field these days is just far too large and the expectation of the public so much greater, that to remain current and give a 'good' service, vets eventually have to specialise. We often have to give up some of the work that we enjoy, but one gets over that!

LA vets dealing with production animals — sheep, cattle and deer — are basic epidemiologists. We deal mostly with populations of animals rather than individuals. We handle epidemics — whether they be trace element or vitamin deficiencies, infectious disease outbreaks, or poor reproductive or growth rate performances. We don't tend to do much curing of individual sick animals because, unless it is a valuable stud animal or a valuable bull or ram, economically it doesn't usually stack up. However, sick animals are still an invaluable source of information and discovering why this animal is not well will often indicate why the rest of the flock or herd is not thriving. One becomes very good at post-mortems.

In fact one of the reasons why I had for some time felt that my future was not in the domestic pet field was because I kept finding my thoughts going down the wrong track when examining an unwell cat or dog. After a thorough physical examination I would sometimes find myself wondering what tests I should be taking. As a diagnostician I was not a patch on PJ or our more recent partners, Stuart Burrough and Mark Wiseman, the shareholders in the practice, but I do know how to do a post-mortem. When confronted with SA cases that stumped me, I kept finding myself thinking, 'This would be an interesting post mortem.'

It was time to move away from small animals and let someone else save them.

So I have had the privilege of sharing a full and eventful working life with PJ. It really has been a great trip and I couldn't have wished for a more stimulating and, at times, exciting business partner. Our friendship has strengthened over time and enhanced our working and social lives, together and with our families. It has also helped us through some difficult periods in both our lives.

Throughout our years in practice together, we would often end the day discussing interesting cases and laughing over some of the more amusing experiences. Whenever an event had us both in fits of laughter, we'd remark: 'That'll be one for the book', never really thinking there would ever actually be a book. Well, here is a bit of a book, but as time has dimmed the memory I know we have forgotten much good material. No doubt some of our clients, if they ever read this, will ask us why we didn't tell the story about 'so and so'. To those people we apologise in advance.

AFTER-HOURS RIPPER — PJ

The great bane of a vet's life is the after-hours work. Getting called out from your warm home when you've settled in for the night with your family is tough. And it can happen at any time, for hundreds of different reasons. You never know what is coming and all country vets in particular will know that horrible feeling when the phone goes. Who is it? What will they want?

As a new vet working for the Graham Vet Club, before Pete and Pete's Pussy Parlour was thought of, I had to face my first night on call a month after graduating.

'Gidday, it's Les Ham. My heading bitch has a bad rip. Can you come out and stitch her up?' The voice on the end of the phone was gruff but not unkind.

I met Les and his friend Bill Gibbs at the clinic half an hour later. I unlocked the door, disarmed the burglar alarm and took the two of them and a nice heading bitch into the surgery. She had a huge rip, from her guggle to her zatch, as the hero of *The Thirteen Clocks* (a book enjoyed by my mother) would say.

'Barbed wire,' said Les. 'Should ban the bloody stuff.'

Les had Clydesdale horses on his sheep and cropping farm in Rapaura, and the sight of four or six of these great beasts in harness with a plough behind and Les on the reins was a joy to behold. Over the next few years I made many calls to see those wonderful animals, mostly good-natured giants, before advancing years made them a bit much for Les to handle. He sold them to various other enthusiasts of his craft, and they were lost forever to Marlborough. He was a lovely, kindly man, invariably polite and appreciative, humorous, and one of those farmer clients I always looked forward to visiting. But all that was in the future.

Back in the surgery, the trusting heading dog allowed me to slip a needle into the cephalic vein and gently inject the anaesthetic. She was asleep in 10 seconds and after intubating her and getting the gas going, I clipped and cleaned the huge skin wound while Les and Bill watched, leaning against the wall of the surgery.

'Would you like a spot?' says Les. I very much enjoy a spot now, but not at the age I was then, and I was new at this and needing to concentrate, so I gracefully declined.

'Well you won't mind if we do, will you?'

Of course I wouldn't. So while these two old World War II soldiers watched and yarned and drank half a bottle of scotch, I went to work, stitching up the great tear in the little dog's skin. These barbed wire rips can be horrendous, and it's sometimes very difficult to fit the jigsaw together. Where did this bit come from? Can I get this bit over here? Use a tension suture or two, Pete. This was one of the worst. Nearly 30 years later, I still can't recall a worse tear. And this was my very first solo emergency case. But away I went and an hour later it was all together again. No more gash. Quite tidy actually. The problem was, one nipple, instead of being just to the side of the midline of her abdomen, was neatly placed up beside her hip.

Now everyone, every vet that is, makes mistakes in the heat of the moment, and especially young, inexperienced vets. One of my friends from vet school went to do his first caesarean section on a cow at about the same time. He correctly opened her up, with the cow standing, on the left side, saw a heap of intestines, panicked, said, 'This is a very strange case,' and closed her up. He went to the right side, opened her up again, found more intestines, panicked harder, closed her up and opened the left side again (the correct one). He delivered the calf safely, but the farmer would have needed plenty of compassionate humour.

My mistake with the dog left me in a cold sweat. 'Oh hell, Les,' I groaned, 'I haven't done that right.'

Les was totally unfazed.

'No worries, Peter. It looks as tidy as my wife's patchwork quilt. She isn't going to have pups anyway. That'll be fine.' Dear man, I could have hugged him in my professional embarrassment.

We waited round for an hour for the bitch to wake up, and I probably did have a dram then. I really can't remember. And as the two old boys took the dog off home and I cleaned up and locked the doors, I reflected on my good fortune in finding such an understanding man.

I saw Les and the bitch numerous times — the wound healed well and never caused any trouble. And I became, if I say so myself, a pretty tidy surgeon, and always paid great attention to the presentation of the finished article after that.

WAKE-UP CALLS — PA

As I retired from small animal practice or, as I tell my colleagues, promoted myself to only doing production animal work, I very quickly became out of touch with veterinary aspects of cat and dog medicine. In 2006 when I was faced with a major health issue, my partners ruled out after-hours and weekend work. This was a very generous gesture on their part because it increased their workload. As it was, I was beginning to feel rather inadequate when it came to doing small animal work because I was only doing it during the odd weekend and after hours.

Being on duty for after-hours calls and weekend work does eventually become a bit of a grind. I suspect PJ would have carried on working for a few more years if he had been able to drop being on duty for 24 hours at least one day a week and working weekends. Unfortunately, with me not doing this work, it would have meant a lot of extra work for the other vets in the practice if he had done so.

In the early days it didn't seem to be a problem. It added to the interest and excitement; it was just part of the job. You also often got to know clients quite well after a few hours with them assisting on some emergency midnight surgery cases. Still, I always found late night calls a bit of a problem because I definitely wasn't at my best when first woken up. Chick grew to loathe midnight calls as well because she knew how I reacted when the telephone woke me from a deep sleep. I just did not perform well.

Calls would often go something like this.

'Hello,' I would answer after fumbling around, sometimes picking up the bedside radio or trying to turn off the alarm clock first. I'd occasionally also knock over my glass of water, which really put me in the right frame of mind to be civil.

'Is that the vet?' A tip: this is not a good way to get a friendly response. Of course I'm the bloody vet. Why else would you be ringing me and I do have a name. Very occasionally I would get an 'I'm very sorry to disturb you' but usually not.

'Yes,' I would reply, or 'I think so'.

'Well, I'm really worried about Tigger.'

'Who the hell are you and who the hell is Tigger?' I would feel like saying. Instead I usually had to ask who was speaking. Not introducing yourself is just plain bad manners. Waking me up when I'm not at my best, asking if I'm the vet, and not introducing yourself: we are off to a very bad start. Chick is by now cringing next to me.

By the time I had found out who I was speaking to, I was usually starting to think a little more clearly and hoping like anything I could find a way of solving their problem without having to get out of bed. Sometimes if I thought the animal could wait until the morning, I would suggest they give the dog a disprin. This didn't always go down well with the dog's owner, nor PJ or Stuart when they had to deal with the problem the next day.

Chick today reminds me of two questions I invariably asked.

'How long has she been like this?' If the problem had only started an hour or two ago and was getting worse my reaction was somewhat more civil than if it had started the previous day.

'What colour are its gums?' That was a good question because no one ever knew and it gave me a little time to wake up further as they went to have a look.

Often, however, it was best to get out of bed and get in the car and drive into town to see whatever the problem was, because if I didn't I would invariably lie awake waiting for them to ring back to tell me that there was no improvement. Our children, George and Caroline, remember the times when I was having a bad night. They would get woken by the phone and shortly afterwards hear me stomping down the hall, slamming the back door shut and then the car roaring off down the drive. What really annoyed Chick was that after I left in what she reckoned was always a foul mood, she would lie wide awake hoping everything was going all right. Then when I returned, invariably now in a good mood, I would fall sound asleep — and she wouldn't.

On the odd occasion there was definitely no need to get out of bed and I could turn over and go back to sleep with a clear conscience that I had done all that was necessary.

I received a call after midnight one night from Greg Mitchell, who had recently acquired a young German shorthaired pointer. Up until then he had been very much a cat person but when his wife walked out on him, she took her precious Burmese cats with her. As she didn't like dogs, Greg very quickly got hold of one, partly I suspect to ensure neither the wife nor the cats returned. Greg, who had always had a fondness for a beer or two, tended to top up more regularly after they left. It was after one of his late-night sessions that he came home to find Neville, his dog, in some distress.

'Pete,' he slurred, 'It's Greg here. I'm really worried about Neville.' There was no need to ask who Greg or Neville were. 'He's all hunched up and uncomfortable and it looks like his balls have slipped down and are strangling his cock'.

'That does sound very uncomfortable, Greg. I'm not too sure I've ever experienced that. Tell me what you can see'.

'Well his cock is all swollen up and red and his balls are not where they should be. They look like they are coming out. Bloody hell, it's horrible.'

By this stage I was getting the picture.

'What sort of look has he got on his face? Does he look in distress?' I asked him.

'Ah, no, no, he looks quite happy actually.'

After I had stopped chuckling away, I explained that Neville had either been dreaming of a bitch somewhere or was possibly very happy to see Greg. He had an erection and what Greg thought were displaced testes was actually the swollen *bulbus glandis* — important erectile tissue that allows a dog to get tied or knotted when mating.

'Go to bed, Greg, and leave Neville alone. Let nature take its course.'

On another occasion telling the owner to let nature take its course was possibly not good advice. I had been woken up at some ungodly hour on a Saturday night by a man who had become worried over the last few minutes because his cat, which was about to have kittens, had not made any progress since she had started to go into labour.

'How long has she been trying to pass a kitten?' I asked.

'At least 10 minutes and she is purring frantically,' he replied. 'I've never heard her purr so loud. Something must be wrong.' He sounded a little anxious.

'And what has she passed so far?'

'Nothing — there's a little blob of whitish jelly stuff showing though'.

'Just leave her alone and go to bed. Give it time. Sounds like everything is in order.'

'But the book says she should have had the first kitten by now.'

'Don't worry about the book. If she hasn't had the first one in half an hour, ring me back. Don't interfere. Let nature takes its course. Goodnight.'

Twenty minutes later the phone rang again. The same man again, now sounding even more distressed.

'She's had the first one but she stopped straining and there are more in there because I can see them moving and none are coming out.'

'OK — what's the kitten doing?'

'It's trying to find a nipple but can't find it.'

'What's mum doing?'

'She's just lying there purring but she's not doing anything.'

'She's resting. She will be OK. Give her time.'

'But the book says...'

'Forget the bloody book. It might be 12 hours before she is finished. Sometimes they take a long time and it's all quite normal. If she strains really hard and nothing appears and she looks as if she is getting distressed then ring me back. Have some faith, man. Have faith that nature will take its course and all will be well.'

An hour later, about two minutes after I had finally got back to sleep, the phone rings again.

'She's had three now but she has been straining really hard and nothing has happened. You told me to ring back if nothing happened.'

'How long has she been straining?'

'At least five minutes. Oh — one minute. Oh, one has just popped out. Oh goodness me. Thank the Lord.'

After lecturing him again on the importance of having faith, I told him to bring her and the kittens into the clinic at 10 the next morning and let me check her. I didn't think about it when he replied that that would be really good because he had an early morning start but would be free by then.

It was only when he came into the clinic that morning with the cat happily nursing half a dozen kittens that I realised I had been lecturing the local Anglican minister on having faith.

A few weeks after PJ and I set up on our own in our renovated house, now a very basic clinic, it was broken into. I was woken by a phone call from the police, who had noticed a door open and realised we had been burgled. The burglars had had plenty of time because they had been through all the drugs in the cupboards, helped themselves to potential useful ones for themselves, stolen our dart gun and then obviously sat around and drunk a couple of bottles of beer we had stored in the fridge. The police were very interested to know what was taken but a lot of the stuff we only found was missing when we wanted to use it and found it wasn't there.

This applied to a drug called apomorphine. This is a very useful drug for inducing a dog to vomit if it has, for example, swallowed a poison. It is a derivative of morphine but has very different effects. It is also a very effective emetic for humans but one of its main medical uses is to treat erectile dysfunction.

Word must have got out among the criminal fraternity that the Anderson and Jerram Veterinary Clinic in Blenheim had some really useful drugs and was a breeze to raid. We didn't have a safe nor did we have an alarm, and it was very easy to jimmy any window or door open in the old house. This was very irresponsible on our part but the budget was tight and security wasn't high on the priority list in those early days. After being robbed it became so. We got a safe and put in an alarm system within a week of being robbed. Two days after the new alarm went in, it went off. We again received a late night call from the police telling us that we had been robbed. On getting to the clinic we found that after they had forced the back door open, they must have been startled by the alarm. They made a hasty retreat and didn't have time to steal anything.

We slept better knowing we had an alarm system in and

didn't think too much about the initial robbery until some weeks later, when a local inspector rang and said he wanted to talk to us about a death we had something to do with. He told us someone in Christchurch had overdosed on something they had stolen from us. The doctors needed to know what it was he had taken, but no one really knew other than it was 'stuff they had stolen from vets in Blenheim'. I'm not sure that overdosing on apomorphine in combination with a horse tranquilliser or two would have been a pleasant way to go, but then again, perhaps there could have been worse ways. While we didn't get any of our drugs back, the police did recover our dart gun, which had been converted to fire live ammunition. Thankfully we never had another break-in.

MOLESWORTH — PJ

Molesworth: the very name is romantic to anyone interested in New Zealand farming.

Molesworth is the biggest farm property in the country, nearly half a million acres of high country at the head of the Awatere, Clarence and Wairau Valleys. The property runs only cattle from the homestead in the head of the Awatere almost through to Hanmer Springs in Canterbury. They have about 2500 mostly Angus cows, roughly 700 heifers and around 1100 steers, although in those days the cattle were mostly Herefords. It's a vast operation in delicate, erodible country with the high altitude meaning long winters and a relatively short growing season. The homestead is at 1000 metres above sea level, and most of the property is higher than that.

The property originally ran thousands of sheep, but a combination of rabbits and the harsh environment saw the last private landowners walk off in the 1930s. The government took over and the iconic Bill Chisholm managed the great run, with cattle only, for the next 40 years, gradually restoring the eroded land. Over those years, hundreds of young musterers from all over New Zealand spent one or more seasons at Molesworth, always a point of interest on their curriculum vitae, although they never called it that.

Run by Lands and Survey, then Landcorp, until about 2000, the property is now owned by the Department of Conservation, who lease it to Landcorp, the government-owned corporate farming company.

Because of my time spent on farms, my Agricultural Science degree from Lincoln College, and my professional interest in soil conservation, when I arrived in Marlborough in 1979 I was well aware of Molesworth and its history. Best of all, it was in the Graham Vet Club's area, and I knew that sooner or later I would get there.

As an aside, one of the vets I worked with at the Vet Club was hard-working, but at times vague and distracted. Dave was once taking a call from Molesworth. They wished to book in pregnancy testing for 600 cows. The call book for farm work always sat on the front counter, and at the same time a client came to the counter and wanted to discuss her sick cat. Dave, interrupted, talked patiently to the woman, then as she left wrote in the day book 'pregnancy test 600 cats'. It caused much hilarity in the practice, not least at the imaginary scene as he tried to hold and rectally examine each cat.

I apologise for the digression.

I had been at the Graham Vet Club for about three months when my chance to visit the famous cattle station arrived. Molesworth had had a problem with fertility in their cows for some time, and in particular, low calving percentages in their heifers, the maiden three-year-old cows. After a lot of diagnostic work, the vets who preceded me at the Vet Club had discovered vibriosis, a disease of the genital tract of bulls and cows. At the time I believe (although I'm open to contradiction) this was the only property in New Zealand with vibriosis, a bacterial condition caused by *Campylobacter fetus fetus*.

A programme of total vaccination of heifers against the disease had been initiated after discussion with the management and with Lands and Survey staff. It was our job to do the vaccinations.

I believe that date was 8 February 1980. In New Zealand, this is the time for the best weather. It is nearly always settled, with large, stationary high pressure zones sitting over the country for days on end.

Marlborough is in a rain shadow, surrounded on all sides by mountain ranges which take the rainfall before the dry winds sweep over the province. Every second year is a drought year here and at times these droughts are serious, going on for several years. As a result, our farmers are careful, conservative people who have learned from hard experience to keep stocking rates down and conserve what feed they have in autumn. With the droughts can come extreme temperatures. Indeed, the hottest temperature ever recorded in New Zealand is still listed as 42.4°C at the Jordan, a property halfway to Molesworth, up the Awatere Valley.

On the day in question, it was going to be hot. A big high pressure system was sitting fair on top of the province as I drove to Marlborough's small Omaka aerodrome. I was being flown to Molesworth by pilot Dave Bishop, in the station's own beautiful red Piper Cub, the best bush strip aircraft for many years.

We took off in lovely conditions and headed up the Waihopai and Avon Valleys, and then through the saddle at the head of the Avon into the upper Awatere. As we went, Dave laconically told me about the properties we were flying over. He knew them all and the people who farmed them and it was a fantastic education on Marlborough for me. Twenty minutes up the Awatere, we flew over the Molesworth homestead, but we were heading westward to Tarndale, a major outpost of Molesworth.

As we came in towards the strip, I could see the cattle yards, full of hundreds of heifers milling around. Men on horses were bringing the last mobs in and then tying the horses up in the shade of some willows. It was very, very hot as I climbed down from the little aeroplane. It was my first meeting with Don Reid, who was in his first full season as manager. Don had worked on the property for some years and had married the boss's daughter, Anne Chisholm. Whether that had been influential in his new appointment, I wouldn't know, but Don was stepping into the very big boots of Bill Chisholm, and it was seen as a signal honour for a young man of 32 to be only the second manager since the government took over the property 45 years earlier. Don subsequently became something of an icon himself on the property, and remains a friend of mine.

He was a very good, disciplined and highly organised manager, who ran a tight ship. He also has an excellent sense of humour, something I only uncovered in later years as I came to know him. But on that first meeting, he seemed stern and serious, and was clearly going to be watching the new vet closely. I got the impression mistakes would be pointed out quickly, and not tolerated.

Also at Tarndale that day was Bill Chisholm himself, along with an old friend, a retired judge from Wellington, but they were up at the cookhouse and were in charge of food.

As I slipped my overalls over my shorts and shirt, I could feel the mid-morning heat already burning on my back. It was going to be a screamer. Don and his men all had big hats, Aussie Akubras, standard stuff on Molesworth, but I hadn't brought a hat at all.

I unpacked my first vaccine pack from the chilly bin and

loaded the multidose syringe. From memory, you could get 20 doses in the syringe. The job wasn't difficult. The men pushed eight or 10 heifers into a long race and I walked alongside, vaccinating under the skin in front of the shoulder. It was important to be precise and accurate as the vaccine was expensive, and the station needed their cows to be protected from the disease. You couldn't afford to miss one.

After two hours in the heat, I was panting. It really was hot, the noon sun beating mercilessly on my unprotected head.

'Dinner time,' said Don, and after emptying the vaccinated cows from the race, I joined the seven or eight men in the walk up to the large hut at Tarndale. A welcome surprise followed. Two flagons of cold beer were produced, and we all sat outside the cookhouse, yarning and rehydrating for 15 or 20 minutes.

Suddenly there came a call from inside. 'Lunch is up' yelled old Bill, and immediately disappeared back inside. In an instant the staff, including Don, were up and racing inside. I followed carefully, not wanting to be pushy on my first day on a new property.

The scene inside was Dante's Inferno. The cookhouse, a hundred years old, and built of the original cob — a mixture of mud and straw — was well insulated. It could be hot or cool as you wished. The problem was the roaring open fire in the old fireplace at the end of the building. On the fire, hanging from big billy hooks were a large camp oven and another great and ancient pot. It was very hot anywhere near the fire. A long table ran the length of the cookhouse towards the fire.

And where was the only spare seat? Right at the end of the table, right beside the fire. Two rows of grinning faces welcomed me into the building.

'You sit there, Mr Pete,' growled Bill, and there was no choice.

Tradition dies hard in the back country and Molesworth is

no exception. Lunch consisted of boiled mutton — ram, I believe — boiled spud and boiled cauliflower, all piping hot from the fire.

I sweated my way through that meal, making polite conversation when talked to, and listening to the high country men talking their own lingo.

It must have been 50°C in there, and by the time it was time to go back to work, I was wringing wet and whacked. It was a relief to get outside, where the mid-thirties seemed positively cool, and I discarded my overalls for the afternoon session. Later, as I packed up and climbed back into the Cub for the trip home, Don shook my hand.

'Nice to meet you. Hope you've enjoyed your first trip to Molesworth.'

Was there a faint glint of humour in the eyes? I never found out but some years later when I was fishing with Don, he well remembered that day. 'Bloody hot, wasn't it?' he said.

THE WORST DAY OF MY CAREER — PA

It seems on some farms, and for some farmers, you can sometimes never get it right. No matter what you do, how you do it, or what advice you give, it is wrong, badly done, or doesn't work. On others, no matter how difficult the situation, how complex the issues, or how critical to the farmer it is that you give the right advice, you get it right every time. You just seem to know that when you return to the property next time you will be warmly greeted and all will go well. I would like to think that more of my clients fall into the latter category. What a pleasure and how rewarding it can be just working with them.

However, when working with animals, always expect the unexpected. You try to cover all contingencies, and the car boot or back of the ute can become loaded with equipment and drugs that are there 'just in case'. Because I often flew myself to jobs, I had to develop a compact and comprehensive surgical kit with appropriate anaesthetics and antibiotics and other drugs for the different species and which covered all basic surgery done on farms — caesareans, castrations, vasectomies, stitch-up jobs, etc.

A few painful experiences, such as a full day manually pregnancy testing cows without gloves or lubricant because I had forgotten to put them in the plane, taught me to run through a check list before I was airborne. Flying in Marlborough's sometimes difficult and windy terrain can, at the best of times, be demanding enough without the extra stress of wondering what you might have left behind. But no matter how prepared you are, something can always go wrong, as on this one tough day on Molesworth Station.

Molesworth Station breed their own replacement hacks and for many years they would do their own stallion castrations — the old-fashioned way, with ropes, knife and no anaesthetic. It had become a bit of a macho thing and each shepherd would get a stallion and castrate and break it in himself. One of the problems was that after weaning, all the colts were run in a group and not handled at all until they were at least three years old when they were then 'broken in'. The other problem was they were big beasts. The manager liked big horses and there was a fair sprinkling of Clydesdale genetics through the group.

The manager, Don Reid, a man for whom I have always had the utmost respect and who had become a really good friend, agreed that it was perhaps time to do it the more humane way and anaesthetise the stallions first. It might pose one or two problems with the yard set-up they had but I had always enjoyed my visits there. If things went as usual, there shouldn't be too many problems that we couldn't sort out. Unfortunately he had to be elsewhere the day we were to castrate the stallions.

Today we have some wonderful new intravenous anaesthetics for large animals, and it is not uncommon for us to use combinations to get a nice even induction, time to do the surgery and ensure a gentle and smooth recovery. The animal lifts his head, stands up and more often than not wanders off for a graze.

The total combination dose required for a large horse can often be given via intravenous injection from a single 20 ml syringe.

However, drug costs are always a consideration and back on this bad day I was using the latest in horse anaesthetics — glyceryl guaiacolate or GG. Although new it was still relatively cheap. It allowed a good deep sedation before the animal was given a bolus of thiopentone to drop it onto the ground. This new sedative's big drawback, however, was the volume of drug required. A packet of powder was mixed with 500 ml of saline and the sedative then given by flutter valve from the bottle and practically given to 'effect'. When the horse calmed down and his head dropped, you could usually stop administering it and push or pull him, even what was a dangerous unhandled stallion minutes before, to a spot where we could give him the magic lie-down brew of thiopentone.

We were to castrate six stallions (they were not colts anymore) in the cattle yards, which really only consisted of a long race, a couple of smallish backing yards and then a large yard further back. To get anywhere near the snorting, extremely wild unhandled stallions to start the job involved encouraging them up the race, getting a 14-gauge needle into the jugular vein in the neck, attaching the connecting tube from the bottle of sedative and then letting it run in. This would take a few minutes and keeping the needle in the jugular vein of a rearing, struggling stallion confined in a cattle race and with a bottle of sedative gurgling in his face had its challenges. Nevertheless we managed the first three with some difficulty.

With the fourth one, the day started to go wrong. He was a big dun stallion and of course the one Don liked the look of most. In the race he was uncontrollable but with the three shepherds helping we managed to restrain him enough to get the needle in and start administering the sedative. By this time I had found that it was quicker to pre-fill half a dozen 60 ml syringes and administer the sedative rapidly (not the best way of administering the drug but at least it was working). In goes the needle, blood flows back out — we are therefore in the vein. Rapidly pump in the first syringe full of GG, reach into hip pocket for the second, horse falls down in the race — dead. Bugger.

Running alongside veins (the blood vessels returning blood to the heart and lungs) are arteries — the higher pressure system taking re-oxygenated blood back to the body, including the brain. All intravenous drugs are given into a vein and in horses it is usually the jugular. By the time the drug, in this case the sedative, has reached the brain via the heart and lungs it has been somewhat diluted. It still doesn't take long to do the circuit and start working. However, if the drug goes directly into the arterial system, especially one that is under extreme pressure from excitement, we flood the brain with a very concentrated lethal bolus of the drug instead of giving it a gentle bathing with diluted sedative. I had missed the jugular and got the carotid artery alongside it. Brains don't like that sort of insult. They stop sending out important impulses such as those that keep the heart beating and the lungs breathing. A brain-dead horse equals a dead horse. Things were not looking too good. The horse was big and dead and wedged halfway down the long race and getting him out posed some problems — and we still had two to go.

All this time I was constantly being niggled by the head shepherd, who kept saying — in what he thought was an amusing way — 'the boss won't be pleased', 'we knew we should have done it the proper way with just ropes', and 'this wouldn't have happened if Dave Sim was doing it'. I was not a happy operator. Somehow we managed the fifth without too much trauma but while preparing to restrain the final colt, my good friend the head shepherd yelled out, 'Ha ha, mate — look what's happened to the last one. His guts are hanging out. What you gonna do now? Never see this when Dave Sim is operating.'

The gelding was standing somewhat wobbly in the yard with a mass of intestines dangling on the dirt. He had herniated through the castration wound. This is nightmare territory. I have one bottle of thiopentone left, one sachet of GG, a litre of saline in which to dissolve the GG, a few swabs, and we have a major emergency on our hands and one dead horse already. I came by plane so I have no spares of anything and the head shepherd is irritating the hell out of me. It is becoming not such a good day.

Action is required. The troughs are full of sludge but the river is close by. One shepherd heads to the river in the ute to collect as much water as possible in the buckets available. The other two are needed to help me restrain the horse before he empties more of his intestines onto the dirt and, worse still, tramples over and ruptures them — a distinct possibility. The first thing was to get him back on the ground under control. More precious thiopentone goes in, an intravenous catheter is inserted into the jugular and hooked up to the last 500 ml of GG, and I give rapid instructions to one of the shepherds about controlling the depth of anaesthesia by taking note of signs the animal is coming around. The kid was good and caught on fast and if he had had another choice for career, it should have been as an anaesthetist.

We have our patient under control, but we have perhaps an hour's surgery ahead of us and only 20 minutes of anaesthetic left, if we are lucky. The water has arrived and is turned into saline by throwing a spoonful of table salt into each bucket. We have no surgical drapes but there is an old tarpaulin on the ute and cleaning metres of intestine onto that is better than back onto the dirt. The worst of the dirt and grime is flushed off the intestines and then, as we feed each millimetre of intestine back into the abdomen, flushed again. There are metres of gut to go, it is a slow job pushing slippery, expanding intestine back up the inguinal canal and well into the abdomen, and we have little time. I snip the opening to the hernia to enlarge it (how the hell did all that gut come out that tiny hole?) to speed things up. The head shepherd, doing the job of manipulating the horse's hind leg and body position to allow easier placement, is still mouthing off. He is told in no uncertain terms to shut up or f... off.

Somehow we got all that gut back into that abdomen and

because of copious amounts of crude saline, relatively clean, repaired the hernia, and covered the horse with a massive dose of antibiotics and tetanus antitoxin. But only just before every last milligram of anaesthetic and sedative had been exhausted. Against all odds, he survived but I cannot recall when we did get around to castrating the sixth stallion.

My good mate Don Reid was naturally not pleased to hear about the stallion that died but he is an understanding man. Colts there are now handled young and castration takes place quietly and easily at the yearling stage.

Any veterinary job with any animal of any species, even cats and birds, can be dangerous work, but the danger both to man and to beast increases dramatically if you have to deal with wild, poorly handled animals. Although today's huge choice of more effective and easily administered tranquillisers and anaesthetics helps in most situations, no vet enjoys working with frightened, uncontrolled and dangerous animals.

PACHYDERMS AND POTATOES — PJ

I hadn't long been in my first job at the Graham Vet Club when the circus came to town. And when the call came to go up and blood test the elephant, my emotions were fear, mixed with excitement. How do you deal with an elephant? I don't remember any lectures. I was there at the Agricultural and Pastoral Society Park, for Blenheim was still a rural servicing town then, in short order, and the elephant trainer gave me the rundown.

This female had been tested in Dunedin recently. She wasn't eating well, and the blood tests had shown a high level of eosinophils. Eosinophils are one of the several types of cells that make up the group known as white blood cells. When you get excess numbers of eosinophils, it can mean an allergic reaction to something like worms, an environmental allergen, or it might even signify cancer.

I think they had treated the animal for worms after the first test, but the great pachyderm wasn't improving.

'We want more blood tests, mate' was the word from the grizzle-headed boss of the circus. 'Brian'll look after you.'

So, trying to look confident, I trudged after Brian, an old stager who looked more like a West Coast fisherman — lived-in face, bulbous nose, and a cigarette permanently parked on his bottom lip.

'Here she is, mate. Hope you can find sumpthin'.' He mumbled the words through the fag.

He picked up a large ebony stick with fascinating brass knobs on both ends. The elephant watched him carefully and when he shouted a command which I couldn't decipher, she grumbled a bit, then got down on her elbows, giant feet protruding forward. He shouted again and she curled the great leathery trunk back onto her forehead.

'Righto, mate, there's the vein on her ear,' he called, then, 'Oi, you do as you're told!' as the elephant moved her trunk towards me.

My heart gave a couple of leaps as I approached the mighty ear. The vein certainly looked big enough. This'll be like the Otira Tunnel, I thought as I attached the needle to the vacutainer holder, put the vacuum-filled tube in it, and pushed the needle gently through the skin over the vein, seeking the lumen, the tunnel, as it were. The elephant squealed in anger. My heart beat faster as I pushed the vacutainer onto the other end of the needle. The blood should flow in now. But it didn't, and as I probed desperately with the end of the needle, she squealed again. The trainer was shouting at her and waving his ebony and brass stick at her trunk and forehead.

I sweated and tried again. A gush of blood squirted into the tube in a moment of great triumph. Brian kept yelling, the beast kept squealing, while the piggy eye was about 10 centimetres from mine, and close to the needle assembly. The tube was full! I quickly removed the needle from her ear and mixed the blood with the anticoagulant in the tube. Quelle relief!

'Good on yer, mate,' from Brian. 'I don't know her too well yet. We got her from Wellington Zoo — she was knocking the keeper round too much.' Thanks, Brian.

We were lucky; the Wairau Hospital laboratory chief had a book on exotic animal blood. The so-called eosinophils turned out to be another type of white blood cells, neutrophils, when compared with the literature. They had looked like human eosinophils, but elephant blood is apparently a bit different. High neutrophils signify an active infection. After a thorough examination of her, I could see she was wincing as she ate. Her lower jaw was swollen. It became obvious she had an infection in her tusk.

I returned later that day with several bottles of sulphur-based antibiotic. Brian shouted and waved his stick, Ms Elephant knelt, put her trunk back on her head and opened her mouth.

'Now, mate!' he cried, and I threw a loaf of bread, impregnated with the antibiotic, into her mouth. She munched and swallowed it.

We repeated the dose daily for several days and I'm happy to report that she came right. Pete A even took a photo of me doing something to the elephant but it's lost, and given I doubt I'll ever get to blood test another pachyderm, a record of this great moment of history is lost forever.

The last part of the story is just about the most satisfying. I used to have a potato-growing contest with one of my neighbours each year. That year mine won easily. I never divulged the secret, but I can now tell you that spuds grown in elephant turds will always outperform the rest. They were real montys. Sorry, Grant.

RACE DAY — PA

Being the only veterinary practice in the area when I first started meant we were always expected to have a presence or be available at most events that involved animals. This included dog shows and cat shows, the Agriculture and Pastoral Show, endurance riding events, and the races, both trotting and the gallops. Some of these events were a bit of a day out and quite good fun, while others could be a drag and not so enjoyable.

One day which I always looked forward to with some anxiety was when I was the duty vet at the races. It was all because I got off to a rather bad start the first time I was 'on call'. Alan did not really enjoy horse work too much and Henk was the boss, so because I was the new boy at the Graham Veterinary Club, I ended up doing the job at the first race meeting in Blenheim after I started practice.

We had a few duties at the track, including checking any late scratchings to ensure they had a valid reason for pulling out, and being immediately available during the race in case a horse was injured. Often a horse, usually the winner, was selected for swabbing by the stipendiary steward. Our job was to escort the horse to the swabbing box immediately after the race and there collect a saliva sample and a urine sample. These samples would be bottled and sealed in a container and later sent for testing to ensure the horse was not running under the influence of any drugs. Sometimes collecting the samples took a while. Getting the saliva sample was not a problem but trying to get an exhausted, dehydrated horse that had just run a race to urinate could be a problem. There were a few tricks we used including rustling the straw in the box, running a tap and whistling. Some horses were great and gave us a sample soon after they came into the box, while others ran through an awful lot of water and caused one to develop very sore cheeks. Being shut in the box with the horse and the trainer and whistling for an hour while a tap ran continuously often meant I ended up very uncomfortable and ready to fill the urine container myself.

After eventually getting the samples we had to be back for the start of the next race, although if we had a reluctant donor we would end up missing the race, hoping that no horse injured itself. Sometimes a horse that the stipendiary steward had wanted to swab was let off because we would still be working on the horse from a previous race. Usually the vet was blamed and the stipe-vet relationship was not always a harmonious one.

David Wood, the Cheviot vet for many years and a great mentor to me, tells a story about one stipendiary steward who really annoyed him by making unreasonable demands, including an excessive number of swabs, having to explain why a post-mortem hadn't been done on a horse and forcing him to work well past finishing time.

In the bar after the race, David had an opportunity to get his own back.

'Did you know that when men are in the shower 70 per cent

sing and 30 per cent play with themselves?' he asked the group, and then turning to the steward asked, 'And do you know what they sing?'

'No I don't.'

'Didn't think you would,' said David.

Anyway, my first day at the races was a memorable one for all the wrong reasons. It wasn't because of the stipe, though; he was a very nice man. Kevin O'Brien, the stock manager at the Vet Club, was also a racehorse trainer, and was in the birdcage during the first race. It was a hurdles race and immediately after the race he came up to me and said:

'You had better get out there. Quick. They are calling for you. A horse has broken a leg.'

'Come on,' I replied. 'Pull the other one.' This didn't happen to a vet graduate during the first race of the first race meeting he has ever been on call at.

'No, look. I'm not kidding. Look out there.'

Sure enough, on the track immediately in front of the birdcage and grandstand stood a distressed-looking horse on three legs. He had broken his leg on the last hurdle and pulled up just before the finishing line.

I raced to my car next to the birdcage, jumped in and shot out the gate and went all of 10 metres to where the horse stood. I leapt out, pulled on some overalls and had a quick examination of the horse. It was a horrible fracture and for these injuries there is only one outcome. It was an easy decision. I raced back to my car boot where I hunted around and finally found a bottle of Euthatal, a very concentrated anaesthetic that we used for humanely euthanising animals, a 60 ml syringe and a large needle. This took a wee while and involved emptying half the car boot onto the race track.

Meanwhile the crowd in the stand had gone very silent. I was on stage and they were watching as I walked back to the horse, filling up my large syringe with 'purple death'. Two groundsmen stood ineffectively with a tarpaulin, trying to hide the horse from the crowd in the stand and in the birdcage. I placed the large 14-gauge needle in the jugular vein and then injected the syringe full in, and then topped up with another one but the horse just stood there. After a few seconds he should have quietly buckled at the knees and fallen down dead. I waited and he just kept standing and standing.

The crowd has just witnessed a young, disorganised vet injecting two syringes full of Euthetal subcutaneously in his nervous haste. That is, outside the vein where it was not going to be very effective for quite some time. I had missed the rather large jugular vein and needed to repeat the act. So I sucked up what was left in the bottle and prayed it was enough. I repeated the job after replacing the needle, this time properly in the jugular, and thankfully had the horse lie down and die next to the sledge placed beside him. It was a nervous moment and not a great way to start being a race-day vet.

Following this I spent a good part of the day swabbing horses and generally being rather busy. The last race also involved a swab and it was well after dark before I had finished. I was invited into the committee room after I had reported in, and offered a very welcome drink. Larry, the head groundsman, was also there and in passing I asked him what he did with the horse that I had had to put down.

'N-n-n-no p-p-p-problem, P-p-p-p-ete. L-l-l-l-yall p-p-p-p—got him.' Larry had a terrible stutter.

'Lyall who?' I replied, suddenly getting an uncomfortable feeling.

'L-l-l-l-yall M-M-M-M-M-M—'

'Not Lyall McLauchlan from the hunt.'

'Y-y-y-y-y—'

'Oh hell, where's the nearest phone?'

I eventually found one and Lyall's phone number and rang him. There was no reply. Now I was really sweating. Lyall was the master of the Starborough Hunt, the local hunt club that had a famous hound pack. They were always on the lookout for meat for the pack and welcomed fresh meat from any source. The fresh meat he had just collected would not do the hounds any good at all.

I kept ringing but still got no reply, so I had to speed out to Lyall's place where the hounds, were kennelled. It was dark and he wasn't in the house although the lights were on. I went down to the kennels where I eventually found him. He was on the verge of feeding the hounds a large hunk of fresh horse meat. If I had been a few minutes later, I would have been indirectly responsible for wiping out the whole of the Starborough Hunt pack. The meat of an animal euthanised with Euthatal is lethal to anything that eats it.

Lyall was not impressed as he had spent a good part of the day collecting the horse from the racetrack and then skinning it. However, he was very relieved that we had not wiped out his beloved hounds. We both agreed we deserved a wee whisky. And Lyall's whiskies were not small.

PONY CLUB ANECDOTES — PJ

I have a confession: I have never enjoyed pony clubs. Horses are not my first love anyway, even though as a young man I rode them in rough fashion in the course of mustering sheep and cattle in the Southland and Otago high country (and enjoyed them in that context). But I've never been really relaxed around them, and a particularly deficient senior lecturer in equine medicine at vet school didn't redirect my energies in any positive fashion. I can cope when I need to treat one, but I don't go by choice.

Pony clubs are not just about ponies, however. Dear me, no. Pony clubs are mostly for mothers, who either want to relive their youth or want their child to do what they couldn't do themselves. The result is a congregation of precious children and anxious, or worse, aggressive mothers on Saturday or Sunday morning. Most vets (not all but most) of my experience stay very clear of pony clubs and I am no exception.

So when my dear wife Ally began to take our youngest, Pippa, to pony club, bought her ponies, horse floats, saddles and tack, clothing and helmets, the reader will understand my apprehension. To Ally's credit, I never had the squeeze put on me to attend. Except once.

For the first year of their equine adventures, Pip and Ally attended a local Blenheim-based pony club and had a lot of fun there. Pip was a natural horsewoman, Ally was determinedly keen, and they began to travel to various places to competitions.

One of the things I treasure most about Anderson and Jerram as a business was the relationship we had with our farmer clients — I have mentioned that most were also personal friends. The Awatere Pony Club, based loosely around the small town of Seddon, 20 kilometres south of Blenheim, had several members whose families were our friends. So it didn't take a lot of persuasion for Ally and Pip to change camps. And because we knew all the families, there came a time when I was persuaded to come along to the end of season Awatere Pony Club camp.

'Just come down for the after match,' said Ally sweetly. 'You won't get caught up in work.'

I forget what I was doing for the day, but I hitched a ride with another family from Blenheim late on a Saturday afternoon in April. We journeyed over the dry Weld Pass on State Highway One, out onto the beautiful Awatere River valley plain, stretching east to the sea, and west up past the majestic Mt Tapuae-o-Uenuku, noted as a 'stupendous mountain' by Captain James Cook in 1770 as he sailed south through the strait later named after him.

We trundled across the rare combined road/rail bridge over the Awatere River (now replaced by a modern structure), through the sleepy township of Seddon, then veered right, up the south side of the river. Twenty kilometres on, this road ends, and almost at the end was the pony club camp.

It was a lovely evening, the air was full of the sound of thundering hooves, happy voices and occasional shrieks of laughter as the mothers had another gin. I talked to some of the fathers, and had a cold beer as we discussed mostly farming and how dry it was. (It's always dry.)

The families were moderately surprised but then, I think, pleased to see me there and at 6.30ish as we were about to head for home, Jim Booth, one of my friends, invited us all to his place for a barbecue.

Half an hour later we unloaded Pip's pony in their paddock and joined the growing crowd at the Booths'. The party was going well, and I think someone had some duty-free high-octane gin. As we munched a delicious venison sausage, the night was still and beautiful.

That was all to change.

'Trevor's crook, Pete.'

It was Jim, and the anxiety on his face was real.

'He can't stand up, and he's just spewed on the lawn. It must be 1080 poisoning.'

I had a good look at Trevor, the family Labrador. He certainly was wobbly — ataxia is the term — and his pinpoint pupils gave me a clue. As I examined him he collapsed and descended into a minor seizure, which passed quickly.

'Is there any 1080 around or have you been using sheep dip?' I queried Jim. He said there had been 1080 put out two months ago, but there was no dip around.

Now, 1080 is lethal to dogs, but even in Marlborough, after two months there had usually been a rain, which would render it ineffective. It looked more like organophosphate poisoning to me. OPs were a very common chemical group used from the 1960s to the 1990s to treat sheep against lice and flystrike. They were a successor to the very nasty chlorinated hydrocarbons, of which DDT is the most famous. These chemicals store for many years in the soil, and worse, accumulate in animals' and humans' bodies forever. They are very toxic, and the new OPs were seen as a saviour. Thirty years later they're viewed as pretty nasty themselves, and have all but disappeared from the scene. But in the 1990s, there were still a few OP dips around.

We'd had a few gins by now, you understand, but my brain was still sharp enough to assess poor Trevor's symptoms.

'I've got to get him back to the clinic and get some antidote into him,' I said.

Jim looked grateful, as did his wife Beryl.

'Do anything you can, Pete,' she said. Jim offered to come with me, a drive of 35 minutes, but he was in no state to drive. Neither was I, but Ally was OK.

We agreed to leave the pony and Pippa with the Booths for the night. Pip was a friend of their daughter and was keen to stay. The pony had a nice paddock so that was fine by Pip.

We put Trevor in the back of the car and Ally drove us to Blenheim. Trevor was very still and looked pretty crook as we traced our way back over the winding roads.

We arrived at our clinic, right on State Highway One at the southern entrance to Blenheim, around midnight. As I opened up the back of the station wagon, a confused Trevor leapt to his feet and bolted into the street, charging along the centre white line. Holy Moses. I sprinted after him, calling for him, terrified a car would come down the road. Two hundred metres on, he stopped, thoroughly confused, then galloped back down the street and straight into my arms.

Hugely relieved, but completely knackered, I staggered back down the road to the clinic. We got him inside, managed to get an intravenous catheter in and began to run in the life-supporting fluids. I found a vial of PAM, the best OP antidote, and injected that and plenty of atropine as well, another antidote. Then I dissolved some acetamide crystals, the antidote for 1080, in another bag of fluid and gave him that too, just in case. I didn't believe it was due to 1080, but I wasn't taking chances.

Later I gave more PAM and more atropine and finally at about 2am when I was satisfied that Trevor would live, we drove home and slumped gratefully into bed.

In the morning, Trevor was a lot better. I gave him another bag of fluids, and more atropine, and the following day he went home.

Of course the moral of the story for me was, don't go to pony club, but there was a sequel which created a lot of mirth.

Some weeks later, Ally was at another social function, possibly connected with pony club. Beryl Booth was effusive in her praise. 'That Pete Jerram is a wonderful vet,' she gushed to the assembled throng. 'He saved Trevor by sitting up with him and giving him *anecdotes* every hour all night.'

We have imagined the scenario many times: 'Now look here, Trevor, don't go to sleep. Did you hear the one about…'

Pony Club Anecdotes | 67

COCK AND BULL STORY — PA

Many of the events I recall readily occurred in my early veterinary days, probably for a number of reasons. Everything we did soon after graduation was 'new'. We were on our own and we just had to make do. We remember many instances well and we learned from them all. One vivid memory involved brilliant diagnostic skills, conflict with the owner, skilful surgery 'in the field', and a patient with a successful outcome. Despite this there was no evidence of appreciation from the patient for having saved his life nor from the owner for having saved his bull, nor from the insurance company for saving them some money.

It was a warm summer afternoon and I was driving up the Wairau Valley in my purple fourth-hand Holden Kingswood to check on a bull that had, I was told, broken his penis. Life was good. This should be easy. The callout was probably just for insurance purposes because apparently the farmer, Mr Fowler, did not often use vets. Even today there are still a few farmers who use vets rarely as they perceive us to be a cost rather than an investment. To them using vets is a sure sign of being an inadequate, incapable farmer.

There was no sign of Mr Fowler or the bull, but the farmer's son, Keith, was there. He knew the story — we were to look at the bull, which was still out with the cows over the hill. Off we went in the farm ute to find a young Angus bull and a handful of cows in heat milling around him. Anyone could tell, even a green young vet, and from a distance, that this was not a 'broken cock' but a prolapsed prepuce. The prepuce, the loose, flexible lining to the sheath which protects the penis but still allows its full extension during mating, was hanging out about 15 centimetres. A tear could be seen, which had resulted in some swelling and the prolapse. This was preventing protrusion of the penis. The more he tried, the worse things were getting. Many a young bull, especially a high libido one, in his youthful enthusiasm will attempt to mate a cow before she is quite ready. An overload of testosterone means power and speed rule, not subtle skills. Leaping onto the cow from a great height, over brambles, through fences and while racing downhill, often with weapon already extended, means there is a good chance of the penis and associated tissues receiving some damage.

I told Keith we needed to give the bull a more thorough inspection before I could sign any insurance document and that I did not think it was a 'broken cock'. He reluctantly agreed to bring the bull in with a handful of cows so the next half hour was spent driving a small group back to the yards. A closer inspection of the bull in the race revealed what I suspected. First dilemma: I can't sign an insurance certificate; second dilemma: what to do. I couldn't just leave it, as it would get worse. A simple remedy for a simple prolapse was a purse-string suture around the prepucial opening to hold everything in until the swelling went down and healing had taken place. But this one was past that stage. Surgery, that is, amputating the prolapse, was the way to go. Great — I was a veterinary surgeon and anything was on, even if I had never done

one or seen one being done. I had read what you did, after all, and I had a kit of sterile shiny new instruments in the boot just waiting to amputate a damaged bull prepuce. I hadn't spent nine years at university and vet school to not use some of my new skills.

So out came the Rompun, down went the bull, out came the antiseptics, local anaesthetic, iodine, instruments, suture materials and, of course, a hefty dose of a long-acting antibiotic. All was going well with half the damaged prepuce neatly cut away and the edges sutured and a good supply of blood over bull, yards and vet. The bull, in a state of peace and tranquillity, was breathing nicely and I was doing what I had spent far too many years at university training to do. Life was good.

Suddenly the peace was rudely interrupted. 'What the bloody hell is going on? What do you think you are doing, boy? Can't you see he's got a broken cock and you can't do anything for that, eh boy?' The bull lifted his head, I jumped, the dogs scampered from the morsels of prepuce and blood, and Keith shut up. His dad was fuming. I don't remember my reply but no doubt I came up with the perfect response — several hours later.

The job did get finished after the boss had stomped off, muttering something about useless young, inexperienced vets just costing money. But the atmosphere in the yard had changed. From feeling I was a healer and achieving great things, I now felt chastised, inexperienced and unappreciated. He had really wanted to take the easy way out by having me write a certificate so he could claim insurance on the bull (the bull was insured for far more than he was worth in the works). However, his insurance covered death, or an injury that meant he was of no further use for breeding. If we did nothing he would never breed again, but we *could* do something and an operation would hopefully allow a useful breeding future. Because of the injury he might not have been accepted immediately at the works, and I could not leave him as he was, with a rather nasty and no doubt painful injury. So I did what I felt was the only thing I could do. But I did learn an invaluable lesson early in my career. Always explain the options, the risks involved, the likely outcome of any operation, whether they be small or large animals, and most importantly make sure the owner, invariably the payer, knows and makes the final decision.

But that is not quite the end of the story. The one who appreciated me the least was the patient himself. Ungrateful bastard — if it hadn't been for me he would have been in several thousand hot dogs in the US. I called in to check on him two or three days later and to pick up my nice new shiny scissors I had left somewhere in the bloody ooze in the yards. I found them and in my delight went into the paddock next to the yards, where my patient could be seen grazing contentedly along with his neatly shaved reconditioned prepuce. From 10 metres away, all looked well.

He stopped grazing and looked at me and then something went 'click' in his tiny little testosterone-riddled brain. Whether it was my smell, the sight of me in my overalls, or just very good bull memory, there was recognition. Usually bulls give you some warning that they are not happy with your presence — they snort, shake their head, paw at the ground, and bellow a bit before making any advances. This one cut out all the preliminary palaver and just went straight into charge mode.

Those who know me would have to agree that I do not have the build of a runner of any sort especially a sprinter, but that day I sprinted. I would have broken any world record for 25 metres if there was such an event. It must have been a sight to behold. But a 10 metre advantage was enough — just. Somehow I beat that bull, now bellowing and getting louder and much closer by the second, to the fence and got the fence between him and me, and God knows how I did that. It was a tight wired fence with the usual couple of barbed wire strands, and those who know me also know I'm not exactly slim, and it was high enough, and high jumping was not one of my strengths either.

There I lay, on the ground, panting and still clutching my nice new shiny scissors. On one side of the fence, a mad bull with a nicely reconditioned reproductive organ, all ready to work next season, but still angry as hell at me; somewhere on my side of the fence, a disgruntled 'cocky' who would no doubt moan about the bill he was about to get.

But life was great — I was still alive.

NAUTICAL MATTERS — PJ

Most Kiwis love the sea. We're all born within 100 kilometres of it, and most of us grow up playing in some part of it. I was no exception. Growing up in Dunedin, we were always in sight of Otago's fabulous harbour and peninsula, even if the waters were cold enough to freeze the balls off a billiard table.

I have strong memories of shivering in the sand dunes at Dunedin's southern beaches, St Clair and St Kilda, as a skinny kid, and for a long time the sea was an ambivalent creature for me — full of interesting things, but always cold.

Our father took us sailing and taught us to row dinghies, and my sister Mary and I would hunt for the large blue crabs around the foreshore of the great estuary of Blueskin Bay, north of Dunedin.

We had a crib (Otago/Southland speak for a bach) there, and I can remember the excitement as the community of Dunedin families who all had cribs at Doctors Point hauled on the large seine net for a catch of flounders, usually with a few red cod and dogfish included.

One night we went fishing in the channel in our little dinghy, long after dark, and I can remember the excitement as Dad told us there was a shark following the boat. Later in my teens, that translated into a very real fear as Dunedin's beaches and harbour were the scene of three fatal shark attacks in about four years. I've never felt very much at ease in the sea since then, but I've come to love being on it. I was given another savage reminder of the perils of the sea when, en route to a tournament with the Lincoln First XI, I was aboard the interisland ferry *Wahine*, which foundered in Wellington Harbour in April 1968 with the loss of 51 lives. Terrified, but in survival mode, I only felt comfortable once I was in the life boat — that was familiar territory, a small boat on the sea.

As a post World War II child, that war and its naval history were very near as well, so when I had a call from a friend to take the First Sea Lord of the Royal Navy fishing in 1981, I jumped at the chance. A delightful man, Sir Henry Leach was happy to don a pair of my scruffy shorts, catch a few small rainbow trout in the Pelorus River, then help demolish a bottle of Chivas Regal. This was all in the same day he'd flown from San Francisco to discuss the sale of some frigates to the Royal New Zealand Navy.

Four years later, Ally and I stayed with Sir Henry and Lady Mary at their home in Hampshire. He got me legless on his home-made sloe gin, while Lady Mary made me promise to have a look at her horse, an Irish Hunter, the next morning. Though I was never better than just competent as a horse vet, full of bravado, I assured her I would be just the man.

Next morning, the tall, angular Lady Mary, aquiline to the point of being equine, purposefully led me to the stable. Her hunter, she told me, had been examined by the horse chiropractor, who had claimed that the animal had three vertebrae 'out'. This has always puzzled me. I was pretty good at anatomy, topping the class in my second and third years at vet school, and I had a reasonable understanding of the intimate and necessarily tight association of the bones of the vertebral column. If there is sufficient trauma to move any one of them out of line, the likelihood is the spinal cord would be severed or so traumatised the horse would need to be destroyed.

The claim that a horse has some vertebrae 'out' when it is standing, walking, eating, interested in all around it, but with a very slight lameness, or even a severe lameness, could politely be called bullshit. The horse industry thrives on this, however, and a large number of charlatans make a jolly good living propounding such nonsense, so who am I, a poor horse vet, to question them?

However, I had dug myself into a hole, albeit with the aid of Sir Henry's sloe gin, so hung-over and out of my depth, I examined the nag, prodded and hummed wisely and eventually proclaimed that it did indeed have a couple 'out' and that it probably needed more visits by the chiropractor, or possibly an acupuncturist.

I consoled myself then and afterwards with the fact that I wasn't registered to practise in the UK and was only giving a visiting layman's opinion. But I have always been a bit ashamed of my capitulation to witch doctor stuff on the other side of the earth.

Six years later in 1991, I had a further close encounter with the sea. A year earlier, I had answered an advertisement in some veterinary correspondence and had spent a couple of days in Wellington training on a MAF (Ministry of Agriculture and Fisheries) officer course for live sheep exports.

Saudi Arabia had been importing live sheep from Australia for quite a few years. The ships all left from Perth, making a 10-day voyage to a port in either the Red Sea or the Arabian Gulf. There were stories of animal welfare problems, and I recall a television documentary about the practice, but I didn't take much notice until I did my own training for the job. In the late 1980s, the trade became lucrative, and some political or trade factors put New Zealand sheep in the sights of the Saudi importers, at the expense of the Aussies.

In June 1991, I agreed to do a trip for a private New Zealand export company, MANZ. They particularly wanted a practitioner from private practice to accompany their shipment, and somehow my name came up. I wasn't that keen. Pete A and I were working hard, we had plenty of debt and there were just the two of us. A month away for me was going to put the business and Pete A under duress unless we could afford to pay a locum to stand in for me. So I negotiated quite hard with Dick Mahoney, a veterinarian partner in the exporting company, and eventually we came to a deal that would provide Anderson and Jerram with enough to cover our expenses and a bit more. I think from memory, it was about $300 a day, twice the government rate and a reasonable sum in 1991.

This was the year of the first Gulf War when Iraq invaded Kuwait. The US took a few months to muster its forces in Saudi Arabia and the Gulf, then struck savagely. The war was over in a few short weeks, with the total rout of the Iraqis, but with Saddam Hussein still in control as George Bush senior put the brakes on, much to the disgust of most of the free world.

My ship the *Al Yasrah* — 40,000 tons, Kuwaiti registered, but staffed by mostly Indian and some Palestinian officers, with a Bangladeshi crew — was to be the first commercial shipment after the war had ended.

I was excited but a bit nervous. My old mate Noel McGirr, a vet from North Canterbury, had been caught up in the previous shipment, some months earlier. As tension developed between the US and Iraq, shipping into the Red Sea and the Gulf came to a juddering halt. The result was that Noel's ship spent eight weeks in the Red Sea waiting for developments and for a place to land the 80,000 sheep.

Noel didn't seem to mind that, but I really didn't want that to happen to me as our business just wasn't big enough to cope with my long absence. So as I boarded the ship in Napier in June 1991 I was excited but nervous.

Loading took two days. A hundred and ten thousand sheep (that's right 110,000), mostly recently shorn crossbred hoggets and a few merino two-tooth wethers, arrived in trucks and were run up into races six decks high, and settled into pens of about 800 each. While the crew, including the Indian First Officer, had done this before, they really knew nothing about sheep.

The pens, only about 1.3 metres high, and much too low for a man to stand up in, were just big enough for every animal to lie down. Along one side of the pens, which ran longitudinally down the ship, were the water troughs. On the opposite side were the feed troughs. The deck was cantilevered so that each pen was angled about 10 degrees to left or right. The idea was that water or any liquid would accumulate on a flat surface, but not on the slope. The sheep defecated on the steel deck and the resulting pad of dung quickly dried, firmed and became quite acceptable as long as it stayed dry.

The problem was that some moron had positioned the water troughs at the peaks of the cantilevered decks, instead of in the troughs. The feed troughs were situated there instead, a ludicrous situation. When it got rough, as it was for the first few days of our voyage, the water troughs spilled over onto the dung pad, which became wet, slimy and, as it got warmer in the tropics, ammoniacal. This very basic design flaw in the sheep decks caused the ammonia levels to become dangerously high.

For the short trip from Perth, in the relatively benign Indian Ocean, it probably didn't matter, but from New Zealand, the ship had to cross the rugged Tasman Sea, then run under Australia, fully exposed to the Southern Ocean. The result had been a lot of ship deaths on previous voyages from New Zealand, and the issue of animal welfare was coming to the fore.

To be fair, a lot of the deaths from previous trips, notably one on the *Cormo Express* where I believe more than 5000 sheep died, had been due to conditions in the tropics. Heat stress, suffocation and high ammonia levels had contributed, but overcrowding was a base cause.

My trip was a bit different. The job of the vet, who was acting for MAF, was to observe, record and report on the journey. Every sheep that died had to have either a post-mortem done or a reason given for its death.

The routine went like this: I would rise at 6am, have a shower, then breakfast in the saloon. By 7.30 I was in the sheep house. The Bangladeshi seamen had by then searched through the pens and were depositing the dead on the companionway beside the pen. On most trips, the deaths were very low for the first 10 days, but on this trip they began immediately. It was rough, force eight to nine, and after passing through Cook Strait and heading due west for Bass Strait between Tasmania and the Australian mainland, we were hammered by near hurricane-strength weather. The seas were huge, with great sheets of water reaching the bridge, 120 feet above sea level, as we ploughed into it. On the second day, the captain, fearing for the ship's safety, bore off a little to soften the pounding, and slowed the ship to six knots, a snail's pace.

The sheep didn't cope well. They had been shorn, fed and vaccinated in the assembly farm in Hawke's Bay in vile, wet, cold midwinter conditions. Many developed pneumonia in the first week. Others wouldn't eat the sheep nuts on offer. This is called inanition — not eating — and the empty rumens of many of the first post-mortemed animals told the story. Anthropomorphising a bit, I believe that the ship's motion had the same effect on them as it does on people before they get their sea legs. They were seasick.

It was rough for 10 straight days until we passed Cape Leeuwin and turned northwest into the Indian Ocean to the west of Perth.

From the beginning, the mornings were spent doing a lot of post-mortems. I eventually did more than a thousand, and that was less than half of the dead.

After lunch (and the meals were terrific, with a choice of Eastern or Western dishes), I would gather an assortment of measuring kit and go to the several measuring stations I had set up around the sheep houses. I measured wind flow, humidity, maximum and minimum temperatures, and ammonia levels at the same sites each day on every deck, and recorded the deaths and their causes.

Then I'd go back to my cabin and put all the data, which I had recorded on a dictaphone, into the official recording sheets. It was a bit tedious, but because the ship was always making progress, there was enough to keep me amused.

Dick Mahoney helped me with the post-mortems on most days, partly to reduce his own boredom, and we enjoyed each other's company. In the evening we would go to the saloon, have a few beers with the officers, watch a movie or read. Sometimes I would go to the bridge for an hour or two.

Of course, this was in the early days of personal computers. The only computer on the ship was in the radio room. They had a teach-yourself-to-type programme so I started on that and by the end of the voyage I could touch type about 20 words per minute, not much but a start.

The time I loved best was on the bridge. Watching the workings of a big ship and the decision making was fascinating. This was before GPS was available commercially. There was an old Sat Nav receiver which would give a position line on which the ship lay, but it took another reading a few hours later to find our exact position by a cross bearing.

The only radar set was old and once we were in the Indian Ocean, where few ships were expected, they turned it off most nights to 'save wear'. I asked the Captain what would happen if a yacht was in our path? He just shrugged. Too bad.

The captain was a difficult and unpleasant character. John Gracias, an Indian, was a difficult man who didn't inspire loyalty in all of his officers. Half of them steered clear of him as much as possible, while the rest did their best to ingratiate themselves with him. The result was that he and his acolytes ate first, then as they finished, the other officers came in and ate separately. It was not a happy ship but it posed a dilemma for the two New Zealanders. We compromised and started our meals half an hour later than the captain so that we could eat both with him and the other officers, most of whom we got on better with.

The deaths mounted as we went north over the equator and into the Arabian Sea: we were losing 50, 60, 70 sheep per day. The merino wethers on the main deck were doing the best. They adapted wonderfully well and it was rare to find a dead one. Of all the complement, they were the group that survived best and made a net weight gain over the voyage.

As we entered the Straits of Hormuz, there was a general buzz around the ship. Iran, who commanded the Straits, was very hostile to the West. An international separation zone on the chart showed very specifically where ships could go, and where they must not go. Apart from the risk of collision with the many oil tankers that ply their seaways, the Iranians were highly likely to shoot at anyone in their territory. Only a few months earlier, US fighters had downed an Iranian airliner, so it was a place of great international tension.

I went up to the bridge at about 1am as we approached the Straits, to see the fun.

To get around the sharp point of Oman, we had to turn 30 degrees to starboard for a few miles, then straighten to port for a few more, before turning sharply to port to get into the Gulf, all the while staying in our own shipping lane.

The first leg was OK. We passed a few ships to port, going the other way, their lights bright and clear. But as the time came for our turn to port, a larger, faster ship appeared from behind, overtaking us on our port quarter. To turn to port would have put us directly on a collision course and a collision of two large ships is definitely something to avoid, particularly with hostile neighbours waiting to pounce.

The duty third officer, a nice Indian named Ross (who had his new bride on board and protected her like Fort Knox, even from our completely civil attentions) became agitated. He called the new ship several times on channel 16, the international calling channel on VHF radio. There was no reply. In five minutes, if we could not turn to port, we would be in Iranian water and in trouble. With a wild look in his eye, the third officer gave the helmsman the order: 'Hard a starboard!'

I could see what he wanted to do. He meant for us to do a complete circle to starboard, a 360, and tuck in behind the faster ship as she eventually turned to port in the Separation Zone. In daylight it would have been relatively simple. But this was a

Nautical Matters | 83

40,000 ton ship in the middle of the night doing 16 knots in a narrow seaway with a dangerously hostile nation waiting for an excuse to cause an incident.

As the big ship swung out of line, heeling hard as she turned to starboard, Ross became completely disorientated. As he came towards the 180 degree turn mark, he suddenly saw the lights of the overtaking ship on our starboard side and ahead in the pitch dark night. The international rule known to all mariners is that ships pass each other port to port when going in opposite directions. Confused and terrified, Ross countermanded his own order and sent us heeling back round to port. It was a frightening moment. A large ship careering around the Separation Zone doing a figure eight, with a panicked third officer in charge.

I watched in awe and some apprehension, and I believe I even said something calming to the panicking officer. As he realised where we were, he did relax and brought the ship in behind the faster overtaking vessel. It was a pretty exciting moment. As we turned to port again, into the safety of the Gulf, Ross turned to me.

'Don't say anything to the captain, will you,' he muttered. He was not one of the captain's friends.

In the morning I had a look at the ship's log. There was no mention of the course change which had nearly caused a disaster. And I didn't tell the captain.

A day later, unbelievably, we stopped off at Dubai, in those days a dirty small dump of a town, to load pails of paint, one at a time from a lighter alongside. It was 40°C and about 95 per cent humidity. Without the breeze created by the ship's way, 400 sheep died of suffocation and ammonia inhalation in about two hours while I raged at the captain. It was completely avoidable. We were only one day's sail away from our destination, Dammam, where the sheep were to be unloaded. It was just one example of the indifference to animal welfare I witnessed many times on that trip.

When we docked at Dammam, 24 hours later, a horde of very young vets came on board. They wanted to blood test 300 sheep for *Brucella melitensis*, a disease never present in New Zealand. To argue with officials in their own country is pointless, but I knew that delay on board would lead to more deaths. I watched these young Saudi vets trying to collect blood. They were pretty hopeless, so eventually Dick and I pulled overalls on, shouldered our way in and did it for them. It took a couple of hours, but it would have taken them days.

Over the next two days, every bureaucratic reason for delay appeared. It was by now 42°C in the shade and 1000 more sheep died in that period, and over the two days of unloading. The only saving grace was darkness falling at 3pm. The thousands of burning oil wells lit by the retreating Iraqis in Kuwait, to the west of us, only a couple of weeks earlier, had created a vast sky full of black smoke. By 3pm it was so dark we needed lights on to work.

There was further drama as I came to disembark. A private soldier waved his AK-47 at me and made me open my suitcase on the wharf in the full midday sun. I motioned to get under the gangplank to some shade but the cocking of his weapon made me think better of it. He took my camera, my film and my skinning knives.

Later in the Hotel Oberoi, in Dahran, I looked out from my window to the hotel grounds. A swimming pool with a few women swimming in it! Now when you've been at sea for five weeks, you do miss female company and just to see a woman is a pleasant change from the all-male shipboard company. I grabbed my bathers, boxers you understand, not budgie smugglers, jumped into the elevator and went rapidly to the ground floor. Military presence was everywhere, a legacy of the war which had only just finished. I approached the armed guard at the door to the courtyard. He stepped in front of the door. 'No, sir.'

'It's OK, I'm just going for a swim.'

'No, sir, now is ladies. Seven o'clock is men.' We really were in an Arab state. Defeated, I plodded back to the lift and went to my room.

A couple of days later Dick and I took a bus to Bahrain, the secular island state in the Gulf. The bus took us 50 kilometres across a causeway, really an eight-lane bridge over shallow water. Halfway across was the border post with Saudi Arabia with a myriad of stretched limousines travelling in both directions. At the border, Saudis in traditional dress disembarked, went into some changing rooms then returned to their limos. But now they were bejewelled, in Western clothes, shirts unbuttoned to the waist, cleavages prominent and burkhas gone. They were off to Bahrain to party.

In the other direction, similarly dressed, exhausted partygoers were doing it in reverse. Emerging in full Arab gear, women properly covered, they had had their fun and were returning to the strict Muslim country of their origin.

I mused. What hypocrisy. How could people be so two-faced? Another of life's lessons learned. Dick and I were relieved to be in Bahrain, got thoroughly sloshed at the airport lounge and headed for Hong Kong.

Afterwards I wrote the required report for MAF. It didn't go down that well. I was critical of the ship, the systems and the animal welfare situation. I said that any New Zealand farmer going on this trip would never send sheep away for live export again. I was asked to change my report, for political reasons, but I couldn't do that. The New Zealand SPCA got hold of it, and I would like to think that changes were made as a result. Not long after, the trade for live sheep exports from New Zealand dried up. It was simply too far to send them on the available ships.

I was asked to do another trip, but declined. For me, the tedium and the lack of animal welfare standards weren't attractive.

This wasn't the end of my affairs with the sea. Soon after this trip I bought our first keeler, and for the next 10 years we sailed around the Marlborough Sounds and Cook Strait, both cruising and racing. It's a marvellous environment and I learnt a lot about myself, and particularly about the weather. As a sailor, you are always watching the weather. I even did one ocean trip on a 40 foot yacht from Hawaii to Tahiti with three friends, a fantastic experience.

I don't know that any of my time on the sea has improved my veterinary skills, but as a relief from the stresses and strains on a practising vet, I can give it my unreserved approval.

MR SCROPE AND TOBY — PA

Some animals with chronic incurable diseases such as diabetes can, at the best of times, be a challenge to manage. For instance with diabetic dogs or cats the requirement for insulin varies with exercise and dietary changes and regulating the dose requires monitoring of blood and/or urine glucose levels. Many pet owners manage this admirably, regularly testing glucose levels, strictly controlling diet, and ensuring they have regular and consistent exercise. Cats naturally can be more of a challenge but I suspect no more than Toby, the little pug dog I had to deal with.

Toby belonged to a delightful old English gentleman, Mr Scrope, whose career in later life had been to purchase horses for the Royal Mews, the Queen's London stables. He retired to Blenheim to be nearer to his daughter but some years later after his wife died was forced to enter a very pleasant old people's home. Toby was allowed to accompany him.

Toby's problem was that he was a diabetic. Unfortunately a common end result of poorly controlled diabetes is blindness. Toby was therefore a blind diabetic dog in an old people's home.

His other problem was that he had an insatiable appetite and while he might have been blind, his nasal passages worked extremely well. Scraps of food can be easy pickings, even for a blind dog, especially one that has spent some time in an old people's home. Blind or not, he knew the best routes to the areas where the clumsiest inmates lived and where there was a good chance there could be some tasty morsels. So we had a blind little pug dog with uncontrolled diabetes, a ravenous appetite and thirst, some incontinence at times, and to top it off he didn't care too much where and when he defecated. Despite significant efforts by the nurses at the home to get the insulin dose right and control his diet, it was really a 'no-win' situation. However, he seemed happy enough.

I got into the enjoyable habit of dropping in most Friday evenings on the way home from work to give Toby a check over. It was a pleasure on my part because Mr Scrope had some fascinating stories to tell about his life and he was a great storyteller. We would sit for an hour or two while he spoke and together we would enjoy a nip or two of one of the very good single malts he had stashed away, Toby sleeping peacefully beside the bed.

Mr Scrope seemed to enjoy the visits as well and he became confident that I knew what I was doing with Toby. I didn't disillusion him with the fact that really there was not much I could do. However, his confidence in my ability to heal grew to the point where one morning I got a ring from him.

'Peter, Peter, I want you to be my doctor. The others are no damned good around here. I have been very poorly for the last couple of weeks and those darned doctors have not been able to make me feel any better.'

'Goodness me, Mr Scrope, I don't think I can legally, ethically or any other way become your doctor. I'm a vet.'

'Of course you can, my boy. You are just as well trained. James Herriot is a very good friend of mine, you remember, and he's as good as any doctor. You have much more effective medicines than they have and I want some more of that medicine I have here for Toby. I have been taking some myself.'

My heart dropped — what on earth had he been taking? I thought it pretty safe that he wouldn't have been injecting himself with insulin, but he had probably been overdosing on Toby's 'choc-drops' — delicious chocolate treats for dogs. I had been bringing a weekly supply for Toby under the strict instructions that he only got a couple a day last thing at night. However, by the quantities he was getting through, either Toby was getting extra helpings or Mr Scrope was also enjoying them. I suspected the latter. Other than choc drops I could not think what he might have been having.

'Mr Scrope, what medicine of Toby's have you been taking?'

'Oh, let me see now. I don't know what it is called. One minute, my boy, I'll just go and check.' I could hear him shuffling around and a short time later he came back on the phone. 'It's thick yellow medicine in the little bottle. It's really good stuff. I have been taking a couple of spoonsful every morning and every evening lately and I am feeling so much better. It really is wonderful stuff. I need some more. I've almost finished this bottle.'

'Ah, Mr Scrope — has the bottle got a label on it? What is it called?'

'Yes, it has. It is called, let me see now, it's called "show-off".'

When I had finished laughing and explained what he had been taking, even he saw the funny side and this lovely chuckle came back over the phone. Twice a day he had been swallowing a spoonful of dog shampoo. Perhaps constipation had been his main issue, and it could have helped, but he sure would have had a shiny bowel.

I managed to avoid becoming his doctor and he did stop taking the shampoo. The choc drops, however, continued their good run.

DEBT COLLECTION — PJ

Vets don't usually make natural businessmen and women. When I went through vet school, we were trained in all things veterinary, but no one told us we were going to be involved in business, which by necessity had to make a profit. So we just assumed that the money thing would be OK, and some of my fellow students even returned after holidays with stories of the vet, in whose practice they had just had free education, 'ripping off the clients' by charging extra for after hours, and charging for euthanising a pet.

There was a feeling that vets were implicitly wealthy and could afford to be generous. The reality, alas, is very different and despite the fact that some farmers, particularly of the dairy variety, still believe that vets 'rip them off' and are fabulously wealthy, I don't know any vets on the Rich List, or even on the Half-Wealthy List. The truth is that we've all had to labour away for many years and very few of us retire with much of a nest egg as a result of purely veterinary labour.

So when Pete A and I started our own business, there was

not just a gap in our knowledge of business systems. There was a black hole, a yawning chasm. And one of the biggest problems was debt collection.

In those days, everyone, regardless of whether we knew them, would charge it up, put their bill on tick, and if we were lucky, they'd pay us next month. I'm glad to say that things are a lot tidier now, but this was then and we didn't want to offend anybody.

Unfortunately one or two of our farming clients and many of our small animal clients always abused the privilege of running accounts, and as we knew them all personally in those days, we took it as a personal affront when someone didn't pay next month, or often for two, three or four months.

Every month our nurse/receptionist Jill would give us both a pile of unpaid bills. We used to pore through them and write appropriate small comments.

'Please, Brian,' or 'We'd be grateful if you could settle this, Liz' etc. We might even stretch to 'Is your arm in plaster?' but not often. Business was very tight and we wanted to remain friends with our clients. It was the strength of our business.

Now there was one farmer, a friend as well, who never paid on time. He wasn't just late — if it was the Melbourne Cup, he wouldn't have been there in time for the clean-up next day. And the bills weren't insubstantial. They were important to us. This particular chap wouldn't pay anyone else's bill either and finally, when he was probably in some straits, he took to passing on all his bills to his accountants to pay for him. But still they were late, doubtless because our account sat on his desk with a heap of others for three months before they were given to the accountant.

After six months of one of these, in desperation, and with some attempt at humorous wrangling, I wrote in veterinarians' scrawl across the overdue account, 'Pay up, you dog tucker.' Now the term 'dog tucker' is derogatory, meant to imply you're not good enough to be meat for the table, but it is also used amongst friends as a form of humorous, put-down greeting. In a very rural New Zealand way.

I thought no more of it, the bill was eventually paid and the matter forgotten.

In those days before personal computers, our wives used to do all of the book-keeping work, and each month Ally would take the assembled debtors' data to our accountants' computer system, enter it all and produce monthly figures for GST. Chick did the same thing for creditors, producing the statements for clients, and then she and Jill would stuff them into the envelopes for mailing.

On one of these trips, Ally's attention was drawn immediately to a familiar-looking statement, nicely framed, prominently placed on the wall of the accountants' staff tearoom. A note pinned above it said something like 'Model of good debt collection technique'.

There, blown up to four times its size, was a copy of the statement (all identifying features removed except the handwriting) we'd sent to our tardy friend. He'd sent it in for payment to the accountant who, highly amused, had decided to showcase it. The problem was that my writing, scruffy at the best of times, had been misread.

They thought it shocking, but amusing. Definitely not fit for the front office.

'Pay up, you dog tucker,' it said. But even I had to admit the 't' looked awfully like an 'f' ...

FLYING AND WORK — PA

In the scheme of things, something like 1200 hours of flying in 27 years, the bulk of it while on veterinary jobs, is not a great deal of flying compared with a commercial pilot. However, many of these hours have been somewhat event-filled. There have been plenty of adrenaline surges. Landing a plane on four or five different short, sloping, one-way airstrips or paddocks in a day with cross or tailwinds is a very different ball game to arriving at a proper airfield with several vectors and windsocks. I have always been full of admiration for the 'Ag boys', who can drop their top-dressing plane on the same metre of strip hour after hour, but they at least are familiar with the strip and can adjust to the flying conditions.

As a young lad growing up on a farm in the 1950s, times were not easy but there was a certain post-war optimism and vitality in the countryside. Compared to today there were a lot more people working in rural areas. In the Hundalees, south of Kaikoura, the main trunk railway line had not been in for long. Groups of two or three railway cottages where the railway workers and their young families lived were set up near railway stations located every few miles along the track. Stock were moved by steam train rather than by road as is done today. They had to be driven along country roads to these local stations where they were then loaded onto waiting stock wagons to be picked up by the next goods train heading down the line.

The hydro-electric lines went through in the mid-1950s and there were many more people, both permanent and itinerant, living in the country. Despite a number of properties being only marginally economic, many were now being farmed by returned servicemen with young families. Most employed a shepherd or two and a married couple. Farming was less efficient and much labour was required just to keep things functioning. Wood for the fires constantly needed to be cut, and while most farms had diesel generators for lighting, there was no power for a refrigerator or electric stove. Although a few TEA Fergy tractors and the odd Land Rover were appearing, horses were still important components of most farms, and needed to be cared for and fed. Oats were specifically planted and harvested for grain and chaff. Scrub was cut by slasher and axe and the land cleared. And of course the cows needed milking at the beginning and end of each day.

Most sheep and beef farms milked a handful of cows to supply milk for the family. Excess was separated and the cream put in the butter can and picked up twice weekly by the 'cream truck', at the same time replaced with a pound or two of butter. The skim milk fed a pig or two and a flock of ducks — the eggs preserved and used for cooking. On top of this there were frequently gangs of shearers, scrub cutters, fencers, rabbiters and road gangs moving through the district. There were more people around and small rural schools were overflowing with us baby boomers. Looking back it was quite a romantic period.

However, nothing fascinated me more than watching the ex-Air Force pilots flying around in Tiger Moths, literally throwing out handfuls of seed and super. The power of a little superphosphate on phosphate-deficient hill country soils was incredible. I had to be a top-dressing pilot.

But I had a wee problem. I also wanted to be a doctor, especially a flying one, because I had heard about flying doctors in Australia, but a guy called a veterinary surgeon came into the district and he saved a sick draught horse, which impressed me no end, so I also wanted to be a vet. I also loved the country and didn't want to live in a city. In the end I guess all my dreams came true. I became an animal doctor who worked in the country and flew an ex-top-dressing plane.

A couple of years after graduating I started to learn to fly at the Marlborough Aero Club. After some stopping and starting caused by financial pressures and a young family, I finally earned my private pilot's licence, but then I had trouble getting hold of a plane. The Marlborough Aero Club was justifiably reluctant to let an inexperienced pilot fly one of their planes into remote farm air strips. It really was a catch-22: you couldn't hire a plane without experience but you couldn't gain experience without doing such flying. The only solution I could see was to own a plane.

I soon became a quarter-share owner in a 90 hp Piper Cub BQX. Although it was a delightful little plane to fly, it was very much a fair weather plane and a bit like flying a leaf in the wind. Don Berry — an older, experienced, laid-back sort of pilot — and I then bought a Piper Colt EEW. Compared to the Cub, this was a rocket but it had a few drawbacks, including being a bit underpowered and not having flaps — which are very nice for landing and for giving more lift on take-off. But I loved it and learnt heaps flying it. Because of its general lack of performance, you had to use updrafts wherever possible when flying in the mountains, avoiding areas where you could expect a downdraft and predicting well beforehand whether or not you could make it over the next ridge. I learnt most by frequently frightening the hell out of myself, but also from talking to experienced pilots or getting them to fly with me. I was able to call on experienced local pilots like John Sinclair and Trevor Collins and very competent 'Ag pilots' David Bishop, Barry Cowley, Andrew Whelan and Ray Patchett. Most of these pilots had spent their life working all over Marlborough and knew the country intimately, and their advice was invaluable.

Mountain flying holds enough dangers even for the experienced and 'current' pilot. And being a pilot who flew intermittently — sometimes three or four days a week, but sometimes not for a month — I could never claim to be fully 'current' even if I was flying the same aeroplane each time. Not being current raises the risk factors significantly. One pilot, Barry Cowley, reckoned it would take him at least seven days of constant top-dressing work, involving hundreds of take-offs and landings, to come to grips with a different Fletcher, even if it was the same model as the previous one. And here I was, flying an underperforming Piper Colt into remote strips, only occasionally, and largely unaware of the dangers. It was Colin Bint, who had watched me flying for a week while he flew a *Country Calendar* camera crew in his helicopter to record the day in the life of a flying vet, who said, 'Pete, that is not the plane for you. Get something with some grunt.' He was so right.

While I always had nothing but total understanding from my farmer clients if the weather meant I couldn't make it on a particular day, there was always some pressure to 'give it a go'. We may have had three or four farms lined up in different valleys and the cows were already in the yards or held close by after weaning. The cattle muster could have taken three days with extra labour brought in and these shepherds were hanging around to help with the pregnancy testing. Another property might also have had the deer in the yards for reading their TB tests, which has to be done three days after the actual test. Going by car would have meant that I could only do one or two of the jobs. The rest would have to wait another day or more. You don't like letting your clients and friends down. If we could fly, we could do them all — no problem.

Pressure to perform, and I hasten to add it seldom comes from the farmer, has meant that I know I have made some unwise decisions in the past and have flown when I should not have. I have not enjoyed those occasions. Flying adds extra stress to the constant physical and mental pressure of veterinary work. There is an awareness of the wind getting up as the day progresses, and the knowledge that the next strip or paddock you are flying to is a tricky one at the best of times. On top of this are the demands of flying in difficult terrain in inclement weather, and time restraints — there are only so many hours of daylight and you cannot fly in the mountains in the dark. There is no let-up and you cannot put yourself into 'cruise mode' for an hour or so like you can when driving. Such conditions can make for a very tiring day.

This may have contributed to a rather serious accident I had in Kekerengu, 70 kilometres south of Blenheim. It had been a big day, starting with an unexpected early morning calving. By the time that was finished I was already late for my planned first visit for the day at Muzzle Station in the Clarence Valley — a 35-minute flight or five to six hours' driving. The jobs at the Muzzle were accomplished in good time but we were still running late. Back to the plane, over the range into the Awatere Valley to Muller

Station to TB test 400 hinds. Things were going nicely but I still had another herd of deer at Kekerengu to test. The pressure came off, however, when Nicky Satterthwaite arrived at the deer shed with a very welcome cup of tea and scones and the message that she had heard from the clinic not to try and go to Kekerengu. The wind there was atrocious and Rod Heard said the deer could wait.

Great, the pressure went off. However, modern technology was creeping into our society and we had the latest in communication equipment — a cell phone the size and weight of a brick. If I flew high enough and cut the motor, I could talk to the clinic and let them know how things were going. Halfway down the valley and home, I contacted the clinic and received the message that it was still a bit windy but not as bad in Kekerengu. Two hours of daylight left, a small group of deer to test, Kekerengu is 10 minutes to the east — let's give it a go.

Despite a good low check run along the airstrip, a narrow strip next to the Heards' homestead, and a contingency plan to land further down the coast at Parakawa if I didn't like the conditions, I must have assumed landing would be OK. Now, the Piper Colt is a 'short coupled' sort of plane. It is like a Piper Cub that has been squeezed from nose to tail and wing tip to wing tip. It is a squat, fat version of the Cub and has totally different handling characteristics. While the Cub will respond beautifully to all control movements at low speeds, the Colt was a bit of a slug. You had to set her up right well in advance and for me landings often involved side slipping with full rudder and aileron movements, a lot of throttle work, and a prayer or two.

It seems I was hit by a sudden severe gust of wind just before touchdown. The outcome in a more responsive plane with more power would most likely have been very different. The Colt was thrown over a row of trees and landed upside down on the tennis court. I have no memory of the accident other than a flashback that still appeared years later of looking upside down at rapidly approaching, neat green grass and me saying to myself something like 'Things are not looking too good here, Pete.' As the air accident report said: 'Game, set and match.' I had written off apparently the second-to-last Piper Colt in the country.

I received a rather nasty knock to the head and several broken bones, including my jaw and several ribs, and was really very fortunate to survive that crash. However, while the broken bones prevented me from getting back to work for several weeks, they did heal reasonably quickly. It was a different story with my knock on the head. The effects from a head injury can take months, if not years, to fully recover from and in my case I believe it took a good two years before I was back to normal. I discuss this more in a later chapter.

Although I loved that little plane, she really was not up to what I was asking of her, but I also believe weariness may have affected my judgement and reaction times.

I needed a plane, so it was back to the good old Piper Cub BPG, this one owned by Molesworth Station but kept at and managed by the Marlborough Aero Club. Although probably the nicest plane I have ever flown, she was still a different plane and we are back to 'the not being current' dangers again. On top of that, hiring planes means you often have to book well in advance and sometimes it is not there even though you have booked it.

This happened one day and was the cause for another close call. Chick occasionally, bravely, flew with me and as this day was likely to be an interesting one, she was quite keen to come along and see some of the country few people have the pleasure of really getting close to. It was to be a full day and there were four calls to make but to our dismay when I got to the hangar there was no BPG. What to do? A full day lined up, four farmers waiting, driving impossible and BPG will be in Nelson for the day. However, Dick Bell's Super Cub was sitting in the hangar. A quick phone call and he kindly gave me the OK to use her.

We were in business. Although I had never flown her she was, after all, just another Cub — or was she? We had the classic danger of not knowing your plane. She had a wee problem with her carburettor, which I wasn't to find out about until the very worst moment.

The final job was to be at Simon and Lynda Harvey's place, Glen Orkney, in the Medway Valley, and I had decided to land in a short paddock below the woolshed, right next to the job. Being mid-afternoon, a good breeze had sprung up. Nevertheless I had a couple of goes at landing uphill with a tailwind but both times had to overshoot. Too much lift and speed and a ridge to climb over at the end of the paddock meant there was no room for error. Try downhill and into the wind. Carburettor heat on, close throttle, full flap, a touch of side-slip. Better, but my technique and the slope meant I touched down too fast and too far into the paddock. Now, the wheel brakes on a Piper Cub are not that effective even at the best of times, and having already used up a good deal of the paddock, I was not prepared just to apply the brakes and hope. There was a fence a couple of metres inside a vertical 200 metre drop into the Medway River and I didn't want to go through the fence and over the edge. No problem — full power on and I'll land next door instead.

Open throttle — nothing but a sort of coughing noise comes out of the motor. Silly boy — you've left the carb heat on. Check: no, it's off. The motor is still not responding, we are only two feet off the ground and the fence and cliff are getting awfully close. We hit the fence at about the same time the motor burst into life and somehow took the top four wires out and kept flying. If I had known the plane, I would have also known she had a problem when full power was applied immediately after a period of having power off. I also would have made sure the problem was fixed. Later I was dismayed to hear that others who had flown her had also thought she had a bit of a problem but nothing had been done to correct it. Not 'knowing' the plane was almost our undoing. It certainly finished forever any small spark of desire Chick may have had for flying with me.

Soon after this a plane I had always desired, and which I felt would suit me admirably, came on the market. It was Ray Patchett's old Piper Pawnee CIQ — one of the classic top-dressing planes. I had to have her and so I bought her. She's a single seater but, if brave, a passenger can sit in the dickie seat with a pop-up canopy, between the motor and the hopper. For its size, the Pawnee has a huge 250 hp Lycoming motor that guzzles copious quantities of fuel, but it performs. I can fill the hopper with half a tonne of equipment and it doesn't know it is there. It was designed for working off rough farm strips and therefore suits my work and has stood up to most of my landings. Some pilot very accurately described flying a Pawnee as like flying a cross between a tractor and a Spitfire.

I had to borrow every cent to buy her and with the repayments, her high fuel consumption and insurance premiums taking their toll, I was forced to lease her out for top-dressing after a year. She came back a little worse for wear with corrosion in the wings, which required a complete rebuild. I was back to the BPG while CIQ (Charlie) was repaired, but not for long.

Piper Cubs love to fly, whether you are there to drive them or not. If you have not tethered them well, they have a nasty habit of becoming airborne on their own when a breeze comes along.

I was on an overnight trip to Mike and Christine Gerard's property in Elie Bay in the Marlborough Sounds, to check some rams and do a few other odd jobs, and then travel by boat to Poehunui for another job. Overnight, unforecast high winds got up — with all the ridges and bays in the Sounds, winds end up arriving in all directions and willy whorls, which are a nightmare to pilots and sailors alike, appear from the most unexpected quarters. Although I had tied the Cub down well in a sheltered hollow, she had to have been hit by one of these. Arriving back to the strip, I could see from the boat that the wheels were higher in the sky than the wings. It was a sickening sight. The tie-down chains and hooks had broken and she had flipped onto her back. For a while I was a rather unpopular figure around the aero club, whose members used to like flying BPG. My big regret is not going in with others to buy the wreck and rebuild her.

Some months later Charlie was flying again. I had wings, but not for long. I had arranged a visit to a client in North Canterbury, 250 kilometres to the south. On the way I was to drop in for a small job at Ward, 45 kilometres south of Blenheim, to see a sick beef heifer at Malcolm Taylor's. There was a mob of sheep on the airstrip, which ran up and along a ridge. These ewes were encouraged to disperse to one side and into the adjacent gully by a low pass over them, and once they had cleared the area I came around again to land. In 1998 Marlborough was in the midst of a drought and to maintain stock condition many had had to be supplemented with grain. Sheep very quickly learn to associate the noise of a vehicle with another good feed. Unfortunately, just as I touched down, three ewes appeared from out of the opposite gully and came straight for me. They obviously thought I was the great grain train from heaven.

The inevitable happened. One got a bit chopped up and

then got stuck in the wheel struts and over we went. Luckily the Pawnee was built to protect the pilot in such circumstances and other than a sore back, I came out of it relatively unscathed. Even if my head took a fair share of the impact, at least this time I was wearing a helmet and as far as I am aware not too much damage was done in that department. However, Charlie was buckled. Another rebuild was required plus a new reconditioned motor — another year with little flying and heaps more driving.

Some self-analysis naturally takes place after these incidents. Could I have done it differently? If I had done another check along the paddock, I might have noticed the three ewes coming out of the gully. If my immediate reaction was to keep the nose up and tail down instead of trying to break and avoid that big fat ewe, I would probably have just driven over her with a bit of a bump. Learning from experience can be expensive. Hindsight is great.

After this incident, Malcolm Taylor really had good reason to wonder about my flying. Some years earlier I had landed on the same strip in the Colt to check his rams. He had a well-known Corriedale stud, and while I was testing the rams we got talking about the next couple of jobs, the last to be at Blairich Station in the Awatere Valley. He said he would love to come for the ride and as it wasn't far out of the way for me to drop him off on the way home, it would be good to have his company. But for some reason — perhaps he had a premonition or a message from a higher power (his wife was an Anglican minister) — he decided as he was taking me back to the airstrip that he wouldn't come as he had remembered something else that had to be done.

When I bumped into him some days later, he said he was sorry he couldn't come for the flight. I had to explain that he was very lucky he didn't. It so happened that the Colt had just had rings replaced in one of the cylinders. Everything started off well but as the day wore on the engine appeared to be losing power. When it came to the last take-off on the Blairich strip in the Awatere Valley, I barely scraped over the fence at the end of the runway. It is not a pleasant sensation trying to be as light as possible and take weight off the seat. I managed to get over the Taylor Pass and make it to the Omaka Airfield. When I explained to the engineer that evening that he better check the motor because the oil had gone very black and she had lost all power, his face went white. He knew instantly what had happened. His apprentice engineer had put chrome rings in a chrome cylinder — a no-no. I suspect with Malcolm's weight as well in the plane we might not have made it over that fence.

A few hours after repairs to the Pawnee were finished, there were more problems. My reconditioned motor started 'making metal'. Not a good sign. Another engine rebuild and more months off flying. I am reluctant now to borrow any other plane and to fly anything I do not know well — I have wrecked enough of them, including my own.

There is one rule I have always followed. When flying you make decisions early and you never change your mind, even if you start thinking perhaps it is the wrong decision. Far better to make the decision to continue to land and perhaps make a bit of a hash of it than change your mind and find it is too late to out-climb the ridge at the top of the strip. Even arriving home 12 hours late once, after a boat trip from D'Urville Island and a truck ride, with a bent prop over my shoulder, was still better than being a statistic on the ridge. Although the strip at Waitai Station is fine on a good day, by the time I had got there that morning the nor'wester had got up and what was a 10 knot tailwind had become a 20 knot tailwind with lots of lift at the point of touch-down. I had committed to land but really had to drive the plane onto the strip. We hit hard and fast, bounced and on coming down again, the prop hit the ground. I wasn't aware it was anything other than a bad landing, until Shayne Amyes, the manager at Waitai, said he didn't know some propellers had 'curly bits at the end'. While I messed up the landing and was annoyed with myself, it was the right decision. Trying to go around could have been fatal. A week later Ray Patchett flew me back in his Cessna 180 with my nicely straightened prop. We bolted it back on and flew home.

THE GALLOPING MAJOR — PJ

It was the middle of spring, usually the very best time in Marlborough. The province sits in a rain shadow, blocked from the prevailing westerly rain by the mountains which lie to the northwest toward Nelson, while to the south the two great Kaikoura Ranges, Inland and Seaward, deflect the regular southerlies out into Cook Strait, and on to Wellington. When it's blowing 50 knots in the strait and pelting rain in Wellington, it's usually a mild, dry southeasterly in Blenheim, or cool and sunny.

But in the spring, all going well, the rains come. The dry brown landscape undergoes a miraculous transformation into a soft, green, productive place of velvety hills and flowing rivers. Spirits soar, and long-hidden cheque books spring out of dusty drawers. New trucks are bought, babies conceived.

It's the key time of the year for Marlborough's farmers, the time when lambs and calves are born, and when feed can be saved for next winter, as hay, silage and baleage. Everyone is happy.

I received the call one afternoon to attend a lame bull.

'He can't move far,' said the farmer.

'Will he be in the yards?' I asked.

'No, you'll need the dart gun,' said the farmer, a retired British Army major who had come to live with his wife on the family farm some years earlier.

The farm was 30 minutes drive to the south, over the winding Weld Pass road, across the Awatere Valley, through sleepy Seddon, then further south over the Lions Back to Lake Grassmere.

This isn't a lake, it's a seawater lagoon, and scene of a famous battle where the great Ngati Toa chief Te Rauparaha nearly found himself in the cooking pot of his Ngai Tahu enemies. He only saved himself by throwing women out of the waka, so they could paddle faster. No metrosexual warrior, he.

The lake is now used for harvesting sea salt, dried by the hot Marlborough sun and processed nearby. Average rainfall is about 350 millimetres per annum, or 14 inches in the old measure.

Now the dart gun is not something one uses lightly. For a start, the drugs you need to knock a bull over in the paddock are very dangerous to use and handle. Vets have been known to kill themselves with Fentaz. There's an antidote but you might not be fast enough to use it if you injected yourself.

It's also a true firearm, a converted .22 rifle, which uses blank cartridges to fire the heavy drug-loaded darts. The darts are tricky to load and pressurise, and at any distance greater than about 30 metres, the darts become very inaccurate as their weight makes them drop. The drugs are also expensive and wasting a dart, which is easy to do, means the vet is down the tube financially. So sedating with a dart gun in the paddock isn't the first choice for most vets.

In the yards it's quite different. Just the confinement of the yards has a calming effect on most cattle. They know they're captured. You can use a gentler sedative, usually xylazine, give it to the bull in the race, then wait for him to sit down in the pen.

I compromised and chose to take the pole syringe, a device you can use from a distance of about two metres. That would do the trick. I thought the farmer was exaggerating. I could cope with a bull in a paddock. I'd done that often, no problems.

It was a lovely spring evening, and I enjoyed the 40-minute drive through green Marlborough hills, a rare but beautiful sight. My heart sang at the beauty of the folded hills, sharply embossed by the late afternoon sun. The paddocks were full of playful lambs and anxious ewes. A good place to be.

When I arrived at the farmhouse I was met halfway down the drive. The farmer was looking worried. He's a good bloke, and doesn't like to put his vets in danger.

'Come in the Land Rover. We'll get as close as we can, then walk over.'

I wasn't worried. I've jabbed dozens of lame bulls in paddocks and then laid them down with the assistance of ropes.

I could see the bull standing alone in the middle of the paddock, as we parked 200 metres away, and at least 100 metres from a fence. Thirty or 40 cows shared the paddock, but he'd lost interest in the ladies, so his leg really was upsetting him.

I loaded the pole syringe and with the farmer five metres behind, advanced confidently towards the bull.

At about 50 metres he snorted and charged straight at us. We were 150 metres from the vehicle, or any other security blanket. We bolted. Now, I'm about 15 years younger than the old soldier, and in those days I still played squash five or six times a week, and cricket every Saturday in the season. I was never very fast but I could get by. As a T-shirt I once saw on an ageing, pot-bellied Queenslander said, 'The older I get, the quicker I was.'

For all that, I made an instant decision to follow the leader and seek sanctuary, but despite his clear start I only just caught the major as we reached the stationary, long wheelbase, flat-decked Land Rover.

The bull was about five metres behind as I turned left and the major turned right to get in the back of the vehicle. The bull obviously had his sights on me as I was closer to him, and he chose my side. As I shot round the rear of the Land Rover, the bull two metres behind, I was astonished to see the major already on the deck. I did another tight full circle of the vehicle before the bull realised he couldn't turn as fast as me and stood there bellowing as, breathless, I joined the amazingly athletic galloping major on the back.

Dave, the farm hand, had observed it all from the other side of the fence, 100 metres away. 'Should've brought the dart gun,' he grinned. 'Never seen the major move like that neither!'

After I'd written this story, PA asked me what happened with the bull. I think he got it to the yards a day or two later and was able to get some antibiotics into it.

DRIVING TO THE JOB — PA

One of the major limitations to the profitability of rural practice, especially in the more extensive sheep and beef-based ones, is the cost of travel. Not only is it an added cost to the farmer but to us the cost of fuel, vehicle and especially time, is significant. Generally vets do not charge travel time but charge on the distance travelled. The returns, however, barely cover the cost of the vehicle and fuel. The cost to the practice of a vet sitting doing nothing but driving is significant. Most rural practices on an average daily basis can only charge out two to three hours, and nowhere near the eight to 10 other professionals might charge.

As a result we try to reduce the cost of travel to both client and ourselves as much as possible, firstly by including as many visits per trip as we can to spread the mileage charged and secondly by not wasting time on the road. Speeding fines are an added cost and not something you can pass on to the farmer.

Choice of vehicle for the job is very much an individual thing. However, when PJ and I first set up practice we could not afford to buy anything. We were really penniless and everything was leased or rented including our building, all the equipment, and the cars. So we had to lease the cheapest cars possible — Datsun Sunny station wagons, which doubled as our family cars. They were very basic machines — underpowered and light, no air conditioning and hardly designed for the loads we took. A big day in the field being shaken around on metal roads could be very tiring. They had to last a few years before we progressed to second-hand Holden Kingswoods, which served their purpose well.

In those early days when they doubled as family cars, we would have to unload much of our equipment to get the family in if we were going on anything more than a short trip. The back seat had to be down for work, so travelling with the family meant some major shuffling of bottles of antibiotics, metabolic solutions, antiseptics, boots, overalls and myriad other tools of the trade. Although we could make room to get the back seat up, we couldn't get rid of the smell. All vets' cars seem to smell the same and we got used to it, even quite liked it, but did the children hate that smell!

Cars for a large animal vet become a mobile office and as he ages it becomes more important that they are relatively comfortable and pleasant enough to drive. We eventually leased new cars which, without fail, created comments from farmers. It was invariably something like 'I suppose I own half of this' or 'You must be charging too much'. I guess it has something to do with the 'tall poppy' syndrome prevalent in New Zealand. One farmer once said to his neighbour when PJ was seen driving his brand-new car, a very basic Holden Rodeo, up a valley: 'You see that man there — he's a vet. I would never get a vet who drove a car like that. He obviously charges too much.' That farmer happens to have inherited a large property, owns a large launch, a European car, and a bach in the Sounds. We enjoy his company but we don't work for him! On rare occasions and now in later years we do get comments such as 'Nice car — about time you had a decent one'.

Punctures can be a real nuisance. In station wagons or cars changing tyres could be quite a performance. Once when driving to Mahakipawa in the Marlborough Sounds, I had a blow out. A nasty nor'wester was blowing and I had to unload the boot to get at the jack and spare tyre. After a day doing farm calls, the boot could get a little untidy with buckets of rubbish and used syringes and dirty overalls lying around. All this had to be placed on the edge of the road along with all my gear. On this particular occasion my box of arm-length disposable gloves was sitting on the top of the heap of equipment. It was blowing hard so I did not take too much notice of the rustling sound until I had removed the flat and was reaching for the spare. To my horror most of my gloves had filled with air and one by one were heading down the road. As far as I could see there were inflated orange gloves with fingers pointing at the oncoming traffic and cars trying to dodge these menacing objects. I got some pretty funny looks as they drove past.

On another occasion, in very much the same place, I had another embarrassing moment. I was hurrying through the hills and had passed several cars. It was early afternoon and I have a terrible problem with sleepiness around 2.30pm, no matter what I am doing. Whether it be driving, sitting in lecture theatres, talking on the phone, doing consultations, whatever — I just get sleepy then. Well I obviously went to sleep. Next thing I woke up with a jolt, having failed to take a corner, and found myself sitting in the mud flats. Luckily recent roadworks allowed easy access off the road and the tide was out. Again I got some looks as the occupants of the cars I had overtaken only a short time previously went by.

Getting sleepy while driving is exceptionally dangerous and I now tend to pull to the side of the road and have a quick snooze. It's amazing how a five-minute snooze regenerates one. There never seems to be any problem waking up because my snoring gets so loud it even overcomes my failing hearing. Unfortunately there's the temptation to push on when your destination is only a few kilometres away. That's when it gets really dangerous.

Once when only about two kilometres from my next job at Kekerengu, 50 minutes south of Blenheim, I 'came to' on the right-hand side of a notoriously dangerous stretch of road, facing a stream of oncoming traffic, the leading car only 50 metres away. I can remember to this day the look on their faces and the rude gestures they gave me. That woke me up. On more than one occasion, however, it has been the sound of gravel on the edge of the seal hitting the underside of the car that has woken me up.

Nowadays the new rumble lines work really well.

I always carry a fire extinguisher in my vehicle and it's come in handy. One day up an isolated country road, I came across a small transport truck with a four-wheeler on fire on the deck. The driver had earlier picked up the bike from the bike shop after it had been in for repairs and was taking it back to the farm. Here he was trying without much success to put it out with a sack and the tea from his Thermos. It really was an extinguisher job. Another time a bird's nest beside the exhaust of a vineyard tractor was burning well and threatening to spread. The tractor driver and several onlookers were not having much joy getting at the fire, but none of them had anything they could use to put it out. Again it was a job for the little extinguisher.

Potentially the worst fire was in my own Holden ute, though, after I had arrived home one evening and parked it in the garage. Prior to leaving work I had filled it up with the following morning's requirements, which included a metal tool box containing TB-testing equipment for deer. In it were clippers and oil as well as tuberculin and tuberculin syringes. The clippers were required to shave the hair off the sides of deer necks. The area would then be injected with a small amount of tuberculin. If a deer had TB, it would react with a swelling around the injection site, which could then be measured three days later. I had placed this metal box close to the 12-volt battery required to drive the clippers. During the drive home, the tool box had obviously slipped across the terminals of the battery. Not long after arriving home I went back outside for some reason, to find smoke billowing out of the garage. A quick check revealed flames leaping around inside the canopy. While I lost some equipment and it took months to get the contents of the fire extinguisher out of clothing and off everything, if I hadn't come outside at that time I suspect I could have lost both the car and the garage. That was a very good lesson and has made me extra conscious of how I pack equipment into the hopper of the Pawnee.

Pete and I have had our share of accidents over the years. I once wrote off my Commodore ute when I ran into a dirty great bale wrapper taking up the whole of the narrow road on a blind rise, and another time I took out a cattle stop. I was running late getting to Weld's Hill, a property at the end of a road off the Medway Valley. As a result I was perhaps exceeding a safe speed, and when I came over a sharp rise found the Holden Kingswood had lost a degree of traction on the shingle. Turning the wheel and applying brakes is a futile exercise when the wheels have lost contact with the earth. Unfortunately, just on the other side of the rise and around a bit of a corner was a cattle stop and when we did come back to earth I was not at all well lined up. I did a lot of damage to the cattle stop and car, and Roo, my bull terrier, was not impressed. He was asleep on the passenger seat and woke up with a start when he was propelled into the dashboard. I still remember the loud grunt he made and funny look he gave me.

Later that afternoon after finishing the ram testing, the Checkleys gave Roo and me a lift back into town. As with many country folk, dogs weren't allowed inside the car but they made an exception for Roo. It took a little persuasion though, to convince them that putting up with his smell and a few of his hairs inside the car was preferable to what would happen to their boot or its contents if he was locked in there.

Pete also had to be driven home by a kindly farmer one night. At the end of a big week transferring frozen merino embryos imported from Australia into recipient ewes on a local stud, all the participants — stud manager, station owner, Australian embryologist, PJ, and a couple of shepherds — felt the need to celebrate their major undertaking. Whether it was the release of tension, exhaustion or dehydration, Pete is not too sure, but something caused him to lose control of his new Mitsubishi wagon. He is actually a very good driver but that night his skills did not prevent his wagon writing itself off on a power pole. It was actually going backwards at 140kmh when it hit the pole.

A large animal vet's car or truck is a mobile clinic, office, communication centre, and sometimes racing car. The problem is they are all too often also where we relax between jobs, reflect on what we have just seen, or think about what we might find at the next farm. Our mind can be in cruise mode as far as driving is concerned, when it should really be concentrating on that very job.

FLANNELLED OAFS — PJ

Cricket is one of the great loves of my life.

From a young age with my elder brother bowling at me at terrifying speed on the front lawn, I was a hopeless cricket fanatic. The first sports book I read was *The Urn Returns* by AER Gilligan, a former England captain, writing about Len Hutton's MCC team in Australia in 1954/1955. The great players of that team became my heroes. My father even took me to see them play against Otago in their short New Zealand tour post Australia when I was six, and I can still recall seeing Cowdrey and May bat together, and our own Bert Sutcliffe caught behind off the great Frank Tyson.

Later, as the first transistor radios arrived, I would listen all night to Ted Dexter's team in Australia, or Bobby Simpson's team in England, and when a relative sent me the 1962 *Wisden Annual*, I was in heaven. I devoured its 400 pages, and before long I could tell anyone silly enough to listen who had captained Warwickshire last year, the scores in the New South Wales versus Queensland match, who took the catches, and of course the score in every test match around the globe that year. In short, I am a cricket nut. The history, the grace, the legends and the tradition around the game still play a significant part in my life.

As a player, I was mustard keen, but only average or perhaps a little better than average. After school I played wherever I was — Dunedin, at Lincoln (hence the *Wahine* experience) on the West Coast, and in Palmerston North during the four years of my veterinary degree, and in many other parts of New Zealand.

When I came to Marlborough in 1979 I had a dilemma. Life had become serious. I was in a demanding job with a lot of nights and weekends on call, and I was a young father. Tom, our firstborn, was nearly a year old. How could I find time to play cricket, and importantly, to practise, because team practice is a critical element of team sport?

A solution soon emerged. The ebullient Paddy Dillon, a local farmer, was keen to put a team of cricketers into the second grade. He rang and organised a get together and a practice. We made two rules:

We would never practise.

If you didn't want to play the next week, there was to be no pressure.

United Country was born, and persisted for nearly 20 years, with the two inviolable rules never broken, to my knowledge. We were a team of cricketers who were all a little older, had limited time, and were mostly associated with rural Marlborough. Some of my greatest friendships emerged from that group of men. We had a tremendous time, went camping as a group with our families, had annual dinners, and even won the competition a few times. We resisted pressure from the Marlborough Cricket Association to play in the senior grade because of the two rules.

At the time, I had to do one weekend in four on duty. In those days weekends on duty were usually pretty light. Dairy farming was not a large part of Marlborough's farming scene, although we did service about 80 factory supply farms in Rai Valley, Mahakipawa and Koromiko, and three or four town supply farms on the plains. These were self-reliant people, and they didn't call a vet unless it was really necessary, so once the spring calving season was over, we didn't hear much from our dairy farm friends after hours.

There might be a horse call or two in a weekend, and sometimes dogs or cats to attend to, but this was before cell phones, personal computers, emails or even faxes. The world was slower, the pace gentler, the populace less demanding for instant service, instant gratification. People were more capable, more able to cope with minor crises, and more likely to fix minor problems themselves.

So even when on call in the weekends, I often played cricket on a Saturday. Our games, 50 overs per side, started at midday and were finished by about 6pm. Any duty calls came to our home phone and Ally, bless her, would take and screen them. If one needed urgent action, she would pack the kids (three by the time PA and I were in private practice) into the car and come down to the park where we were playing. I would see the old maroon Austin Westminster pull up, and I would realise that I was needed. It didn't happen too often, sometimes once a game, sometimes not at all, although Ally remembers one afternoon with four calls when she was not best pleased.

For some calls, I could get Ally to ring back and arrange for them to meet at the clinic at 3pm or 6.30pm depending on the urgency. Farm calls generally meant immediate action because of the time involved to get there.

One Saturday in November, the team had assembled at Horton Park. We changed into our whites under the trees, and had a few hit-ups and catches. We were fielding first, and as we walked out to start the game I saw the familiar maroon car coming round the corner.

'There's a deer having trouble fawning,' said Ally.

'Who is it?'

'Colin Wells.'

Oh hell. Colin farmed at Nopera in the Keneperu Sound, a good two and a half hours' drive away.

'He said he'd meet you at Te Mahia in his boat in an hour,' Ally continued. This was better. Two hours' travel (an hour each way), an hour to do the job, I'd be back in time for a bat mid-afternoon.

I took off through Renwick, north across the Wairau River to Havelock, then turned right on the winding road to Linkwater. Left here, over the hill to Mahau Sound, winding, winding on a gravel road and eventually to Te Mahia in the Keneperu. One hour exactly, and there was the ever-smiling Colin in his fizz boat at the jetty. In five minutes I had my kit packed in the boat and 10 minutes later we were unloaded and in his deer shed on the north side of the sound.

Colin and Mary Wells were real Sounds farmers, self-reliant, kindly and generous. They had sheep, beef and one of the first deer farms in the Sounds.

While Colin held the hind's head in a narrow race, I lubricated my hand and gently inserted it past the protruding front legs of the fawn. It was large and the head and long neck were turned back. The natural position for fawns to be born is like a spring board diver, front legs and head extended forward, but this one wasn't playing the game.

It was a common problem in the first few years of deer farming, as farmers came to terms with the hind's feeding requirements. In the wild, constantly foraging for their food, the hind naturally limited the size of the foetus, but on a farm full of high energy spring grass, the fawn could grow very large and the hinds over-fat. The combination led to many cases of dystocia, difficult birth, and led to a lot of vet call-outs.

I cleaned my hands and reached for my kit. Filling a 2 ml syringe with local anaesthetic, I gently felt for the spot at the base of the tail and injected the drug into the epidural space. In five minutes, the tail and vulva were relaxed and flaccid. Now I should be able to get my hand in far enough to correct the angle of the neck and bring the head and the other foreleg out.

Alas, it wasn't to be. The fawn was large, the hind very fat, and the birth canal diminished as a result.

'It's no good, Colin. We'll have to do a caesarean,' I volunteered.

Now Colin and Mary had to make a decision. A caesarean section would cost a lot. On the other hand, in those days, a hind had a value of up to $3000, a lot of money in the early 1980s, and a live fawn, close to $1000.

'Well, you're here, let's do it,' said Colin.

So there and then we did it. I sedated the hind heavily, lay her on her side, then clipped her left flank in a long vertical stripe. I washed and cleaned the area, injected local anaesthetic just anterior (toward the head) of my incision line, scrubbed my hands, draped the wound area, and made the first cut with sterilised instruments. In a few minutes we were into the abdomen. The glistening pink uterus was obvious. It was important to bring the uterus out through the incision in her flank, so that when I cut into it to extract the fawn, the fluids from inside the uterus could not flow into the abdomen. If they did, a fatal peritonitis would be the likely result.

Carefully I put both hands around the warm pink uterus, and gently manipulated it out through the hole. I laid more sterile drapes all around the area that the uterus would lie on, and when satisfied, I carefully incised the lower, gravity-dependent surface. A whoosh of amniotic fluid shot out and down onto the floor of the shed. Reaching into the uterus, I found the two hind feet, and protecting the uterus from their sharp edges, I gently pulled the little animal out, all long legs and long neck, and laid it beside the mother. Instantly it began to splutter and Mary cleaned its mouth and nose. It would live, a moment of pleasure and triumph. Then came the hard part. First the uterus had to be sewn up with a special suture pattern to invert the serosa, the external surface. And it had to be watertight so nothing would leak from it. Then after washing the now shrunken organ with warm sterile saline, I replaced it in the abdomen.

Three more suture layers were required, one for the peritoneum and the three muscle layers, one for the subcutaneous tissues, and one for the skin. By the time I had carefully and neatly completed all of that, the hind was stirring. Colin removed the jersey from around her eyes and we rubbed some of the fawn's amniotic fluid around the mother's nose, hoping that it would help her to accept her fawn. Sometimes after contact with man, they won't, and the farmer is left with an orphan fawn to rear.

I picked up all my gear and the fluid-soaked drapes and retreated. Best to leave mother and fawn to sort out acceptance or not.

'You need a cup of tea.' Mary, kind Mary.

'Thank you, Mary, but I'm in a bit of a hurry.'

Colin knew I was a cricketer, and a keen sportsman himself, understood the situation.

Back to the boat, we roared across the Keneperu Sound to Te Mahia and I hurried off back to Blenheim. The day was disappearing as I pulled up at Horton Park, but the teams were still on the field.

As I got out of my car, someone hit the ball and ran a single. Players on both sides shook hands and began to walk off the park. The match was over. I was too late.

It was a lesson. From that day on I rarely played if I was on call. It was too tough on Ally and frustrating for me. And it probably meant I gave less than brilliant service to our clients. These days, with clinics open seven days and a public which demands service to a much higher level than it did 30 years ago, it is simply impossible to play sport and be a vet on duty.

But they were great times, and I continued playing cricket for a long time. I was 60 when I played my last game and I think I can claim the last *Wahine*-sinking injury. Our ex-Lincoln Wahine Survivors team went to Queenstown in 2008 and played in the International Golden Oldies tournament. We were really well past it, and it became embarrassing as we hobbled and shuffled around the field. In our final game at a beautiful ground in Clyde, I set off for a single. There was a bang as my Achilles tendon snapped. I knew my cricket career was finally over. These days I just watch, but I'm still just as passionate. It's a beautiful game.

ALTERNATIVE MEDICINES — PA

In one weekend I became an expert acupuncturist. I had another string to my bow and I was anxious to use it.

I had spotted an advertisement for a basic course in Nelson on acupuncture for animals and as I had always wondered how this Chinese needle trick worked, I was interested to find out more. The weekend involved sticking needles into some long-suffering greyhounds, a bit of theory, something about yin and yan, and an acupuncture instruction book. The book had very good diagrams showing the specific acupuncture sites to place the needle for, say, a sore shoulder or an arthritic hip. It didn't seem to matter what the problem was. I used the same acupuncture points for a recent sprain as I did for chronic arthritis. Equipment was minimal, just a packet or two of acupuncture needles.

After some extensive practice at home one evening on Roo, our bull terrier, who found the whole procedure a bit of a joke, and once on Chick, who didn't, I was Peter Anderson, Veterinary Surgeon and Acupuncturist, and ready to use my new expertise.

I stuck needles into many animals to treat anything I thought was treatable with acupuncture. Many cases were chronic arthritic-type lesions where there had been limited benefit from the conventional anti-inflammatory drugs available at that time, so we were often starting with difficult cases. To my amazement I occasionally got a response. I started with dogs and seemed to get some results but found cats very unrewarding. Horses also amazingly seemed good subjects. Obscure conditions such as 'sore backs', which were often unresponsive or only temporarily so to conventional anti-inflammatories or corticosteroids, sometimes seemed to respond to a couple of treatments of acupuncture. I had one or two successes and my reputation spread. Two people didn't have to be asked if they would like me to give their animal acupuncture. They actually asked me!

However, I'm not totally convinced they always asked for the true reason.

Early one afternoon David Gardiner, who had a busy cleaning business and trained a few trotters, asked me to acupuncture a horse with a 'sore back'. It can take a while placing the needles at the recommended sites but horses seem to tolerate them well as long as you get them in the right spot. If you don't, a flick of a tail and half the needles are lost in the bedding of the stall. So tying down the tail is an important precaution. Anyway, David starts complaining that he is working too hard and can't sleep at night. For some reason I knew the acupuncture sites for insomnia. Not for animals, as insomniac animals were not in my repertoire of diagnoses and treatments. I placed and left a couple of needles in his hand while I twiddled with those in the horse and thought nothing more about it.

I rang David a few days later to check how the horse was and whether it should have another treatment. However, he gave me the impression that for now acupuncturing was disallowed in the Gardiner household. It transpired that after I had treated David for insomnia he had gone home to change, sat down and fallen asleep. A full afternoon's work never got done and he did not wake until his angry wife stormed home at 6pm, wondering where he had been all afternoon.

Encouraged by my success, I also gave Fred Rouse the insomniac treatment at the same time I treated his dog. He had a favourite old cocker spaniel gun dog bitch that had had an earlier elbow injury. The joint was now badly arthritic and I felt acupuncture might help. Fred thought so too. The idea was to give the dog three treatments, once weekly, see if there was a response, and go from there. The acupuncture did not seem to help the dog — but Fred kept coming back for his. After the third visit he rather embarrassedly said that really the only reason he was coming back was that his wife forced him to. For the first time in 30 years of marriage, he had slept all night without tossing and turning and moaning and groaning and keeping his wife awake. I gave Fred a couple more treatments. I'm not sure how he sleeps these days.

Another afternoon I went to see a trotter with an obscure near hind leg lameness. The owner was not there but his wife and daughter showed me the horse and we examined it in the usual manner. It was one of those cases where the horse was slightly lame at times and never when the vet was examining it. So it was difficult to isolate where the pain came from to cause that lameness. Acupuncture to the rescue. I was placing the needles in the strategic spots, which because I felt I needed to cover all areas and joints, included several in the troublesome hind leg. As I said, horses tolerate needles very well — as long as you get the specific acupuncture sites. I guess I got it wrong. The kick was fearsome. It lifted me up and threw me against the far wall of the stall.

I slid to the ground writhing and doubled up in agony because the bastard had got me where all men fear to be kicked. Through the pain and tears I could see the woman and daughter looking very awkwardly at each other, wondering what they should or could do. There really was not much they could do.

I gave up acupuncture after that.

The last laugh had to come from PJ. He had always been a little cynical about my interest in 'alternative medicine'. One weekend about 10 days after the big kick in the groin, he and I went for a fish in the Sounds. It was a beautiful, calm, sunny afternoon and time for a dip. After I had discarded my clothes, PJ started to laugh. Other than a small pink bit at the end of a certain appendage the whole of my lower abdomen, groin and upper thighs was a deep purple black and some areas were also swollen. A very impressive sight. Even today when I go past Blumine Island in the Queen Charlotte Sounds, I still hear his laughter.

There is definitely a place for acupuncture in veterinary medicine. However, it is a time-consuming process requiring patience and perseverance. The response to a treatment, or course of treatments, may not become apparent for some days to weeks. Invariably any response is not as spectacular as that which we expect after the easily administered shot or course of today's drugs, of which we have a huge arsenal. Those who do it well find it a rewarding skill and I admire their perseverance.

DEER THINGS — PJ

ervus elaphus. The red deer. The name might not mean much to some, but to those in the deer industry, and to passionate old hunters, it has a mighty ring.

Pete A and I were lucky enough to do our early vetting during the very beginnings of deer farming in New Zealand. These were hugely exciting times. Many New Zealanders of that era were past or present hunters of red deer in the wild, but few had handled live animals up close, and our knowledge of their health problems was basic, and at the very beginning of a new dawn of knowledge.

Red deer are not like sheep and cattle, which have been domesticated by man for centuries. Deer have a massive flight reaction, and a very long accepted approach distance, especially approach by humans. As a result, we had some pretty exciting, and at times, damned dangerous adventures in our dealings with these beautiful animals.

Deer were introduced to New Zealand for sport. As early as 1840, the first deer arrived in Nelson and were liberated into the rugged and wild bush country which covered so much of the country. They quickly adapted to their new home, a wonderland of green culinary delights, vegetation which had evolved for thousands of years in the absence of browsing or grazing mammals. Further releases in Canterbury and Otago enhanced the quality of the antlers, which sportsmen sought so eagerly. By the mid-1920s while species such as fallow, sambar, rusa and whitetail had established in various pockets, it was the prolific red deer which adapted and multiplied the best.

A release of North American elk, or wapiti (a gift from US president Teddy Roosevelt) was made in wild Fiordland, and these great beasts, a close relative of red deer and able to interbreed with them, soon became famous for their trophy quality heads.

Until the 1970s, deer were wild animals. In fact it was illegal to keep them in captivity. The Department of Internal Affairs regulated this strictly, and the first applications by the helicopter hunters of the 1960s to farm deer were quickly rebuffed. That was because the deer had become pests. Their huge success in breeding had endangered our native forests and alpine grasslands, a fact recognised in the 1930s and 1940s. Training programmes were devised to produce hunters, or deer cullers, whose sole employment was to kill as many deer as possible. Huts in remote locations throughout the back country were built to give refuge to cullers, and many tracks were cut and swing bridges built to give access into the very rugged country where the deer lived.

In the 1960s came the helicopters. After decades of fighting a losing battle against the deer, here was a solution. A hunter in a helicopter would shoot several hundred deer in a day. Working in conjunction with a man gutting the carcasses, thousands of deer could be processed and frozen in a week.

An extraordinary export trade, mostly with Germany, emerged and flourished. Gradually the helicopter operators realised that if they captured and farmed these wild animals, they could grow bigger and better, and could supply the world at any time of the year. A major added attraction was the production of velvet antler by stags. In the course of growing their antlers each year, stags produce a rapid-growing velvet-covered fleshy, soft antler. This product was, and still is, hugely valued for herbal medicines by many oriental countries, especially Korea.

So the leaders in the helicopter business began to pressure the powers-that-be to allow deer to be farmed in captivity. I was involved in the first application to farm deer on the West Coast in the 1970s. A committee of no less than 12 representatives of numerous government and local authorities inspected the site. I have no idea what we were looking for, but bureaucracy was still rampant (it was a bloody sight worse than now, although many have forgotten and believe it is bad in 2011) and someone must have believed that captive red deer could spread pestilence and disease to other farmed animals.

The upshot was that in my first year as a veterinarian, deer farming was extremely new and as I have said, we had to pioneer all sorts of practices to handle them and manage their animal health problems.

The first aspect was handling facilities. It was found that captured deer settled best in the dark. The result was that every deer shed in the early years was so dark that you had to stop and let your eyes adjust for several moments before you could see anything. Then there was dust. And in many cases there still is. A roof over the top, enclosed walls, bare earth floors, dirt-covered hairy animals, all added up to dust. After two or three hours working in a deer shed, I would develop a cough that sometimes lasted a month. Sedating drugs were also a problem. The early drugs for capture, barbiturates and opioids, are dangerous for the operator and for the animals.

As deer became domesticated, Rompun (or xylazine) was found to be adequate to sedate animals for velvet removal, for minor surgery or even tuberculosis testing in some cases. But even xylazine is hugely variable in effect and numerous deer have died while under the drug's influences.

On many late spring evenings, Pete or I would be called to a fawning. We'd load the dart gun and head for Rai Valley, 45 minutes away, where our first deer farm clients were. Their deer sheds were primitive, and with hinds and young fawns in the paddock, mustering the herd in was impracticable. We loaded darts with Fentaz and sat in the passenger seat or on the back of an old Land Rover or Toyota truck as the farmer drove through the paddock towards the hind in trouble, a head or two legs protruding from her rear end. It was hugely exciting. As a mad keen hunter, I loved seeing deer, and the excitement of being close to animals I'd shot in the wild for years was pure heaven and all adrenaline. You had to get to within about 20 metres to accurately shoot the heavy, drug-laden dart, powered by a .22 blank. A lot of to-ing and fro-ing usually ensued as the farmer would try and manoeuvre into range.

'Now!' Crack! As the dart got past 25 metres, nearing the end of its range, you could actually see it, before it reached its target, as the projectile slowed down. The aiming point was muscle in rump or neck but a lot of darts hit deer in every part of their body.

I once shot at a hind who turned right around as I fired. The dart stuck in her right rump despite my firing at her left. It was a sheer fluke but the farmer thought I was Kit Carson. If the dart stuck, we'd back off and wait for up to 20 minutes for the hind to lie down under the influence of the drug. It was pleasant to sit in the beautiful bushclad valley, waiting and talking with the farmer.

When she was down, we would approach carefully until close enough, and someone would dive on the hind's neck and hold her. Then I'd get to work. The long neck and long legs of newborn fawns can make the birth process extremely difficult. In a normal presentation the head and two front legs come first. If the head or either leg gets bent back, they won't slide through the birth canal. And it's tight in there. A man's hand is a huge addition to the crowded pathway, and you would have to attempt to push the head or legs back in, then try to get all three forward. It is very difficult and we had to learn to develop new techniques for epidural anaesthetic, for loops to secure the head with one hand inside the hind, and especially, develop methodology for caesarean section. No one had performed C-sections on deer before and while the surgery itself isn't especially complex, the anaesthesia and after-care of these volatile and delicate animals was all pure learning for us.

Stags were another matter. They are big, extremely powerful, and during the roar or rut (the breeding season) their normal fear of man all but disappears, making them extra dangerous.

I once had to TB test 100 stags for one of the Rai Valley farmers. TB or tuberculosis is a lethal, slowly developing bacterial disease which infects the lungs then the whole body. Worse, it is transmissible to man. A national scheme to test deer for TB is now firmly and successfully in place, but in those days we had to devise our own schemes.

These stags were stroppy. It was early winter, not long past the roar and they all had hard buttons of antler where their velvet had been harvested. These buttons above the permanent pedicle are bone hard and two of them protrude about 10 centimetres above the crown of the skull, between and behind the ears.

First I had to clip a bare patch on their necks to have some relatively hairless skin to inject the tuberculin into, so that three days later we could read any swellings as a positive reaction to TB. Clippers are now mandatory for this job but in those days we used scissors.

Nobody had a deer crush or any other devices to secure the animals. The only way to keep the animals still enough was to pack 30 or 40 stags tightly into a dark pen and just wade in amongst them. The stags had shaggy manes, full of dried mud from wallowing during the roar and by the time I'd clipped 30 I had large blisters on my thumb and first two fingers. The farmer, Murray, would try to hold the stag more or less in one place while I clipped the neck and injected the tiny dose of tuberculin into the skin in the centre of the clipped patch.

It was a nightmare. Every 20 or 30 minutes, one stag would object to our presence in his vicinity, and without warning would thump his head, complete with antler stumps, into my kidneys. It was only the crowded nature of the pen which prevented them from getting a run-up first and really doing me some damage.

All veterinarians of that era will have experienced this

scenario. We all did it. And because we were young, fit and hugely keen, it didn't seem too bad, even though we knew we had to go back in 72 hours and 'read' the same stags. This entailed viewing and palpating the shaved patch for any sign of swelling, the dreaded positive for TB. The reading was, at least, mercifully swift, and with correspondingly less chance of injury.

On one occasion, Pete Anderson came home with a nasty hole in his face, immediately below one eye, where a spiker, a young stag, had prodded him with the tip of its young antler. Two centimetres higher and Pete would have lost the eye.

On another occasion, I was velvetting two wapiti bulls. Wapiti are large, almost twice the size of a red deer. A large male weighs in the vicinity of 400 kilograms. And they know it. If you got too close in the yards they would start to grind their teeth with a sort of ominous 'click, click'. The tongue would protrude out of one side of the jaw, and their eyes would roll back.

The owner, a professional manipulator of human bodies, was present, but not actually in the pen. He always wore white gloves when handling his deer, although I never found out why. When the deer were dangerous he was usually on the other side of the wall.

I approached one of these two great beasts with the pole syringe, a device which gave me about two metres' reach, with a spring-loaded mechanism releasing the sedating drugs when pushed into the animal's rump. The first bull was no problem. I approached quietly and slowly, talking gently to the animal as I came within range. Brian, the farm manager, was behind me as back-up. I pushed the loaded syringe into the bull's rump. An explosive kick into the plywood wall. The bull dashed round the corner of the pen. I'd got him! A moment of relieved triumph. He'd be down in five or 10 minutes.

The second bull wasn't so easy. 'Click, click, click . . .' His head was up, tongue out, eyes rolling, saliva dripping from his angry mouth.

As I came within range and reached the pole towards him, he charged. In a confined space, 400 kilograms of angry wapiti is not a pretty sight. I retreated, facing him with the pole held out, but he wasn't stopping. He reared above me on his hind legs, smacking great blows at my head and shoulders with his front legs, as I tried in vain to wedge myself into a corner made by the swinging door. I was in big trouble. One of those blows could kill me. Showing great courage, Brian ran into the fray and walloped the bull across the rump with a broom. The bull turned to face this new foe, then dashed around the corner of the pen. I climbed shakily over the wall to safety.

Another episode soon forgotten, but one of many close calls we had in the early days as deer veterinarians. Since then, things have changed. Everything has to be super safe.

I've always believed the general drive for life without risks began with the Fireworks Lady, a woman whose child had suffered a bad burn from fireworks in the 1970s. This daunting person began a one-woman crusade to rid the world of fireworks, eventually presenting a petition to parliament. Obviously, it didn't completely stop fireworks but it encouraged a lot more people to speak up about matters of personal safety and soon we had bicycle helmets, codes of conduct for innumerable workplace practices and finally the dreaded OSH.

However, deer sheds are one place that have changed for the better. We now have crushes, races, concrete floors for less dust, and catwalks around the pens above the animals so they can be directed or drugged without danger to people.

It's all good but the old days were much more exciting.

ROO — PA

I don't think many veterinarians would be in the animal business unless they actually enjoyed working with animals. However, I always found one of the standard statements people would make when they found out I was a vet, 'Oh, you must love animals,' a little naïve. What can you say in reply? Sometimes after a kick or a bite I didn't feel much warmth at all to certain members of the animal kingdom.

In my generation of vets many of us grew up on farms. Animals, including sheep, cattle, horses, dogs, hens, ducks and a cat or two, were very much part of our lives. Those that didn't grow up on a farm often had relatives or family friends with farms and so had some appreciation of the farming way of life. Times have changed, and now many veterinary graduates enter employment with very little understanding of what actually happens throughout a year on a farm other than what they learn during the limited compulsory farm practical work in their early student days. Regardless, most vets do enjoy having animals around them and whether or not we 'love' them is not the issue. Life would just not be as full and rewarding without them. As a result most of us have a family pet — or three.

Unless we go for a parrot or an elephant, we tend to outlive our pets. When one pet passes on and the grieving process has taken place, most people get another. We remember them all but for many people one particular animal often stands out as the 'best' or most memorable. For my family it would definitely be Roo — a tricolour bull terrier.

Soon after I started practice I had a bull terrier come into the clinic. He had a rather horrible skin condition, not uncommon for the breed, so he needed some antibiotics and a couple of injections including a vaccination. Bull terriers cannot be described as delicate or pretty. They are a solid beast with little beady eyes in a wedge-shaped head containing immensely powerful jaws. They have a short coat and prick ears and just look tough. Anyway, this dog sits on the table and takes all I give him. Skin scraping, scope the ears, finger up rectum to check his prostate, squeeze the anal glands, a couple of injections. He just stood there — tail wagging and with a silly grin on his face. I was impressed. I had to have one.

So we got Roo. Roo was a black pup with a white brisket and lower legs and some brown on his head. He grew up with our children, Caroline and George, arriving just before Caroline was born. He was a constant part of their lives when he wasn't doing the odd farm call with me. He would play with them when they wanted to play and be their pillow when they wanted to rest. Despite his looks he was a calm, good-natured dog and incredibly strong. Both George and Caroline learnt their rudimentary riding skills on him.

Roo often came with me on farm calls. Sitting quietly upright on the passenger seat of the Holden station wagon, he would scan the road ahead and to the side, interested in everything that went past, a constant grin on his face. He never complained. He was a good passenger. Farmers and their dogs, after their initial shock when he jumped out of the car, soon got used to him. Despite his appearance and his breed's reputation, he was not at all aggressive. He was a pacifist in the dog world. Farm dogs seemed to accept him as something the vet brought and a bit odd but not a threat. Anyway, Roo was more interested in finding things to eat and he wasn't fussy.

Depending on what the sheep had been eating, their faeces could be a delicacy. Fresh cow pats were worth a lick or two as well, but best of all were bits of some animal that I had removed previously and failed to dispose of. He would never wander too far from where I was working and by the time I had finished the job, he would often be waiting for me by the car, ready for the next call and potential gourmet delights. However, he didn't always wait by the car. If it was a hot day and I had left the windows down, he could clamber in. Not being that agile meant the paintwork on the car door was ruined by deep gouge marks. If he had had a particularly successful scavenging experience, I would have to put up with a rather unpleasant odour for the rest of the day.

I started to have second thoughts about enjoying Roo's company on farm calls when one hot summer's day, while checking a large line-up of cows on a dairy farm, he decided to wander into the settling pond next to the shed. This held the putrid contents of a few years of faeces washed daily from the shed. It had a sort of crust over the surface and weeds grew on it. Roo could be forgiven for thinking it was a nice smelly grassy area to investigate but he wasn't forgiven for what he did next. After breaking though the surface and floundering around for a while, he extracted himself and then, caked with a black, sticky, foul mess, went straight to the car. What better place to clean himself up than on my seat? He was definitely not a popular dog that day.

I always enjoyed stopping for a cup of tea or lunch while doing farm calls. In the early days it was a good chance to get to know the farmer and family better and you always picked up valuable information and learnt things if you had the time. However, if I suspected it was going to be a very full day and there wouldn't be any spare time, I would grab a sandwich or bread roll when heading out of town and usually eat it later while driving between calls. A fairly unhealthy way of living but needs must. Needless to say Roo, on more than one occasion, helped himself to my lunch while I was away from the car. If I had hidden it well, he usually couldn't find it, but that wouldn't stop him trying. Clambering into the back of the station wagon, he would fossick around amongst overalls and equipment and drugs. Once he came across some plastic bags of freshly collected and carefully prepared post-mortem samples, including bits of intestine, liver, and kidney. Oh, what a feast.

Roo once made himself very unpopular with Ally Jerram. One summer evening our two families camped beside the Onamalutu stream, a small but pretty tributary of the Wairau River. It was a lovely evening and while the children played by the stream watched by their two young mothers, PJ and I started to assemble the tents under a nearby willow tree. Roo, anxious to help with the tent poles, had to be removed from the scene. We bundled him into the back of PJ's Ford Escort vet van. We didn't think much more about it, and didn't even question why he looked so contented, and slightly bloated, when we released him after the tents were assembled. It was only the next day when Ally went to get the two large quiches out of the chilly bin in the back of the van that we realised the error of our ways. She had gone to considerable trouble preparing this lunch the day before and now all she could find were two empty trays — both licked clean. I don't think Ally ever forgave Roo. We were a little annoyed as well, having to go without lunch.

It was also a memorable camping trip for other reasons. We had not been in practice together for long and that day PJ introduced me to fly-fishing, a pastime I have enjoyed since but far too infrequently. I introduced him to parsnip wine. He has never forgotten or forgiven me for the hangover he suffered. However, neither Roo nor I ruined forever the friendship that was starting to blossom between the two families.

Next to eating, Roo's greatest joy in life was playing with sticks — the bigger the better. He would dare people to take sticks off him and loved being swung around on the end of a large one.

He was hard to shake off. On the odd farm when he got a bit bored and there were no morsels around and no sticks to play with, he would start ripping battens off fences. They could be a challenge but were the perfect size. Once he had them he wouldn't want to give them up and once tried to take one home, chased by the somewhat amused farmer. Unfortunately for Roo the batten was far too wide for the car door and he was brought to an abrupt halt.

Digging holes was another passion. He didn't do too much digging at home — the beach was the place and there he was in heaven, with lots of sticks and logs and children and birds to chase. He would knock over small children as he raced around with huge hunks of driftwood and undermine the sandcastles of others. On one occasion we left him contentedly digging his way to China but got a little concerned when he turned up with an elaborately carved but rather mauled walking stick. Apparently he had lined up a very old gentleman tottering quietly along the beach and hit his walking stick at considerable Roo speed. The poor old fellow didn't stand a chance and was sent skittling. Although a little shaken, he was very gracious when we returned the stick to him.

Roo filled our lives with humour. Sadly he developed lymphatic cancer when he was around 12 years old and despite some reprieve from chemotherapy, we eventually had to put him down.

FAECAL FACIALS — PJ

Spring is a wonderful time. The days are longer and warmer, trees which have lain dormant for months are springing to life, the grey of winter is changing rapidly to healthy, vivid green. Newborn lambs appear beside their anxious mothers and play wildly in groups in the early evenings.

For veterinarians in rural New Zealand, spring also means something else — calving. Calving a cow in difficulty can be a satisfying and uplifting experience, or it can be difficult, rotten, smelly, and very, very time consuming. Not just that, a large proportion of calves are born at night, so a call on the home phone at that time of year can raise the blood pressure by a few degrees if you happen to be the vet on duty.

But this was a midday call on a Sunday and it was close to town, only 10 minutes' drive towards the sea. The Boyce brothers milked about 200 cows, grew cash crops and fattened a few store lambs — a typical Marlborough low country property of the 1970s and '80s.

Alas, today all that land bears grapes. The animals have gone.

Row after terribly neat row of vines have replaced the livestock. Winding flax-lined streams have become dead straight, cleanly battered and sprayed drains, devoid of stream life.

But I digress. I drove down the valley, with that all too familiar, 'What will I find here and will it take 10 minutes or three hours?' feeling. When you're the only vet on duty, long jobs usually mean there's a list of callers waiting for you at the end. And we didn't have cell phones then.

The Friesian cow was already in the pen and the brothers pushed her into, then locked, the head bail. I gave her an epidural anaesthetic, carefully injecting 5 ml of local anaesthetic into the spine at the base of the tail, lubricated my hands and had a feel. Tight but probably manageable with a good pull.

I slipped the calving chains onto the two forelegs still inside the cow, and attached my calving rope (an ex jib sheet from my old yacht) to them. At the other end I made a turn around a post, then fashioned a 'truckie's knot' to double the leverage — a sort of bush pulley.

'I'll steer it through, you guys pull as I call it,' I said, with an authority I only partly felt. The brothers pulled. I lubricated the calf and even stood on the rope to increase the traction and to give it some downwards motion. This one was really tight.

'Pull guys,' I urged.

The head was protruding through the vulva, but it was a big head, and it didn't want to come. I tried to lever the offending skin over the calf's head. The brothers pulled on the ropes. The head was moving out!

With a noise like a squawking pukeko, a powerful jet of cow shit burst from the cow's rear end, hugely pressurised by the calf's head just below it. The jet caught me midway between the eyes and spread over my face. The calf shot out, and I eased it to the ground, expecting some help from the farmers.

I looked up to ask for assistance, but I was wasting my time. The brothers were rolling on the ground, howling with uncontrollable mirth. The sight of the vet's face covered in cow shit was far more important just then than the calf.

'Jeez,' said the older brother, 'we'll call you out again. Now let's see if we can get this calf breathing.'

DROPPING BULLS — PA

Being one of the more valuable animals on farms, bulls tend to make up a significant proportion of our work. Often it is to check them for mating soundness. This involves testing their ability to successfully serve a cow, blood testing for infectious diseases, and sometimes collecting a semen sample to test quality. Bull testing is done routinely on young sale bulls on stud farms and on the handful of mixed-aged bulls on commercial farms. Who should be culled and who can be retained for another year is an important decision to be made before the autumn bull sales.

The other common job is to trim feet or attend to a foot abscess. Lame bulls do not tend to work too well and it is important they are sound before the mating season. On most jobs with bulls, it's best to start with heavy sedation. An aggressive or nervous bull can be a dangerous animal and sedation not only makes the job, whatever it is, safer but you tend to do it better. A bull is a heavy beast as well, and unlike the other heavy animal we deal with, the horse, is invariably untrained.

One of the problems we have to deal with when making a

diagnosis in the field is that to examine an animal thoroughly we may have to tranquillise it. Unless a handy means of restraining an animal is available, such as a good set of yards and a head bail or crush, then we often have to 'drop' it. Not all vets have the same procedure but you tend to stick to the one that works best for you. A common method is to run the bull up a race and inject it in the tail vein with xylazine. In about a minute its head drops, it starts to drool, and then it often urinates. It will stagger around and then lie down — but not always. This vein, a relatively narrow vein running along the underside of the tail, is easy to miss, especially on a moving target. Missing the tail vein means the tranquilliser takes a lot longer to work, sedation is not as 'deep' and ropes to help restrain the bull may be needed. But even when they do drop easily, different beasts respond differently.

On one occasion the particular bull appeared sufficiently sedated but after we placed the rope and applied some pressure, he decided it was time to leave. He smashed through the stockyard gate and dragged Jim Allen, the farmer, and me out onto the farm track. Jim bailed out but I was determined not to let go, hoping the tension would finally bring him down. Jim dined out for weeks on the vision of me bounding after the bucking bull hanging onto the rope and disappearing down the track. On this occasion, giving up meant hours getting an agitated bull back to the yards and starting again. In the end I had to, and came back to retrieve my rope and finish the job a few days later.

Another time I was working on what appeared to be a well-sedated bull. I was working on an abscessed hind foot while the farmer, Robert Oswald, sat on his shoulder chatting away, when the bull somehow brought his foot forward and took out Robert's two top front teeth. They sat out at right angles to his face and I'm sure at the time he reminded me of Bugs Bunny. While the sight of Robert was rather amusing, it was serious enough. We managed to force the teeth back where they looked like they belonged and Robert tells me today that they are as good as they ever were. The little incident luckily didn't spoil his good looks.

We can usually get around under-sedation by giving bulls more of the tranquilliser. However, overdosing with the drug has its problems. Nowadays we have access to antidotes to most of the tranquillisers, which can get around the problem to some degree, but this has not always been so. At Upcot Station, I was testing all the bulls for a venereal disease, which involved collecting washings from their prepuces (the lining of the sheath of the penis). The race in the yards was not a particularly easy one to work from, so I had decided it would be best to tranquillise them all first and let them all go down in the yard and collect the samples as they lay there.

So we filled the race up with half a dozen bulls and I worked my way down, giving them all an intravenous injection in the tail. After I had injected the second, I asked Bill to open the gate and let them out. Thinking all would be well, I carried on injecting. Unfortunately the first bull had decided he didn't want to move through and out the race. Before we knew it, the tranquilliser had started to kick in and from not wanting to move, he now doesn't care if he moves or not. He just wants to go to sleep. Next thing bull number one is down in the race and before we could back the others out the fourth bull went down. So we had two bulls wedged in the race and between them two more steadily becoming more sedated. Eventually we had four bulls down and wedged in the race and, apart from dismantling a substantial construction, could do very little until they woke up.

While it is best to work with bulls in the yards, we sometimes have to make do in the field. They may be a long way from the yards or are so lame that driving them there is painful and unpleasant for the bull. In those cases, we use a pole syringe, a syringe attached to a piece of dowel or aluminium pole, or a dart gun.

In 1990, I was into doing a *Country Calendar* programme. I guess having a vet flying to work was a bit of a novelty. I thought it would be quite an experience but while I wasn't too sure how my speaking bits would go, I was more concerned that all the practical veterinary stuff would turn out all right. We arranged to do several farm calls where we had a number of jobs lined up. But for some reason very few of the procedures that I thought worked brilliantly, and which would have even impressed one or two of my colleagues, were never aired. We castrated a colt, vasectomised a stag, post-mortemed a ram. These all worked brilliantly and I made some very profound statements during them about all sorts of wordly matters. It was so good I even impressed me. None of this was shown. Instead, anyone who remembers the programme only remembers Colin Nimmo and me chasing a mildly lame bull through the briar and brambles on his property, Muzzle Station in the Clarence Valley.

Muzzle Station is one of the more remote properties in the country, lying in the Clarence Valley between Muller and Molesworth Stations to the west and the Seaward Kaikoura mountain range to the east. Access is via a long, narrow, winding road from south of Kaikoura or by air. Colin manages the property with great skill using his Cessna 180 or Robinson (R22) helicopter. So we flew by helicopter to this lame bull, holed up in his comfortable little dell in the scrub. However, he was not going to have anything to do with two men with a pole syringe, a cameraman with a huge camera on poles, a soundman with a big hairy sausage on the end of a stick, and the programme director with a big excited smile on his face.

Our arrival was all too much for the bull and he was off. Colin reckoned his lameness had improved significantly and we both knew immediately that we were not going to get anywhere near him. We very quickly gave up the pursuit. But while we thought we were wasting our time, Chris the producer insisted we carry on. Eventually we persuaded him that it really was not a very fruitful exercise, us scrambling through the scrub and the bull getting further and further away, and we were sorry we had cost him a good part of the afternoon and a lot of money. However, I was surprised at how delighted he seemed. 'No, no. It was great. You did so well. The scenery is brilliant and we got all the action. And I know just the music to play with it.' When it was aired the background music was the toreador song from *Carmen* and I did think Colin and I were made to look a little inept. However, we are not the ones that make the decision about what appeals to the public, and obviously things going wrong are more interesting to TV viewers than when everything goes nice and smoothly.

TRUSTING FRIENDSHIPS — PJ

It's fair to say that one of the great defining features of the practice that PA and I built up over nearly 20 years was the relationships we built with our farmer clients. The majority of them were not (and still are not) just clients. They were and are our friends. We've been to their parties, their woolshed openings, some of the weddings of their children, and of the farmers themselves. It's something we're proud of and cherish.

Being invited into a client's home is a privilege, and also an opportunity to find out what makes him or her tick: what they like, how they live, their politics, their attitudes. An old farm advisor told me when I was a student at Lincoln College in the early 1970s, 'Never say no to a cup of tea,' and he was right — well nearly so.

So when I finished the pregnancy testing of a few cows at Ross and Chris Beech's property, at the end of a one-way road in the Awatere Valley, I was delighted to accept the offer of a bite of lunch.

Now pregnancy testing or PD (preg diagnosis) is a dirty job. Your overalls are usually pretty well caked with cow shit, and I was careful to take them off at the back verandah and leave them out of sight before I entered the lovely old farmhouse Ross and Chris had refurbished in the 15 years they'd been on the property.

Ross and Chris are special friends, also from Lincoln days, so it was no trouble to spend a bit too long over lunch, and suddenly I was late for my next call, back down the Medway road. I thanked my hosts, grabbed my boots at the door and bolted down the dusty road. Only at the Awatere corner, 15 minutes later, did I realise that I'd left my overalls, but I had a clean pair in the car and carried on with my day.

A week later, I'd clean forgotten the overalls, when Ross came into the clinic with a paper bag in his hand.

'You might want these,' he said in his gruff manner.

His manner might have been off-putting but I knew my man, and after a look at the cleaned, ironed and folded overalls in the bag, I was effusive in my gratitude. In fact I was quite touched. No other client in my memory had washed my overalls, and ironed them too, so it was a special moment.

Later I put the overalls in the back seat of my car. I had some cows to test for the Griggs that afternoon. After lunch I drove cheerfully up the Taylor Pass Road, not far from Blenheim. The hills were dry and dusty, but the day was fine and I was going to see more good clients, even if I didn't know them all that well in those days. Now they are friends, and they became people I really enjoyed visiting. But this was earlier in our relationship and I was minding my Ps and Qs. Tony Grigg was half a generation older than me and I'd always been a bit nervous of him, but with his son David there, half a generation younger, it should be OK.

Tony and David were waiting as I pulled off the road and drove across the bare paddocks to park near the yards. Brian, their farm worker, was there too, a kind and friendly man.

The cows, about 200 or so, milled in the yards, and I knew I would have a pleasant couple of hours testing them with my gloved arm in the rectum of each in turn. With good company, pregnancy testing was a nice job — dirty, but when you were fit for it, not too strenuous, and as another farmer once said, you could 'put your mind in neutral and carry on'.

The Griggs and Brian came over to the car as I got out and reached for the beautifully folded and ironed overalls. I shook them out and climbed into them, then glanced at my hosts, who were all gazing in wonder at my now overall-covered backside. I twisted my neck and could see a beautiful patchwork flower, sewn neatly onto the bum of my overalls.

Trusting Friendships | 161

Bloody Beeches! Ross can't sew but Chris is an expert weaver, so I knew who'd done what. It would have been Ross's idea though. The Griggs were amused and enjoyed the joke with a bit of ribbing as we walked over to the yards. I was amused but embarrassed.

Back at the car, I'd pulled some shoulder-length gloves out of the box, with a roll of tape to hold them on, then stuffed them into the pockets of the overalls.

As David and Brian went back to the filling pen to load the race with more cows, Tony stood by to help me tape my gloves on. As I pulled the first glove out of my right pocket, a Durex Featherlight condom, neatly packaged, fell from the pocket and landed at the farmer's feet. He bent down, picked it up and looked at it. 'I think this is yours,' he said non-committally.

Bloody Beech. He'd double got me. I tried to explain.

'Bloody Ross Beech,' I muttered, but Tony had turned away to watch the cows trundling up the race. He never mentioned it again, even years later when we sailed together on a friend's yacht for two or three years. So I'm sure he didn't believe me.

But he is a very polite man.

FLYING AND PASSENGERS — PA

There are some marvellous quotes about flying. Nevil Shute wrote in *Slide Rule*: 'To put your life in danger from time to time... breeds a saneness in dealing with day-to-day trivialities.' And Antoine de Saint-Exupery: 'I fly because it releases my mind from the tyranny of petty things...' or as someone else once said: 'Flying is the most exciting thing you have ever done with your pants on.'

I found that there was no time to dwell on the job just finished or to think too much about the next job when flying between properties. One should concentrate fully while flying and as much of our veterinary work requires full concentration as well, there is often no let-up during the day. It can be tiring. However, I suspect only those of us who fly really understand the feeling of euphoria one experiences when doing so — particularly if it is a calm day. Once you have the bug it is difficult to get it out of the system and you just need to fly. At times I know I have been guilty of forgetting that family and partners and staff at work also worry when I am flying, and I neglect their concerns and fail to keep them informed of progress during the day.

You do not miss too much from the air — as long as you are not too high. Everything from the air looks different. The countryside looks neat and orderly and looking down everything seems to be moving at a slower pace. So much of my flying has been done on a high, with many memorable days.

One warm summer evening on returning to the airstrip at home, I passed over a property of good friends. Aidy leapt out of the swimming pool and raced around waving her bikini top in the air. We both circled around the pool a couple of times — she at ground level and me a couple of hundred feet up and getting lower. She has a glorious figure and so I just had to have a swim too. I landed amongst a couple of horses, dressage arena, and practice jumps in the paddock next to the house and had my swim. Word got out about my impromptu swim and a couple of weeks later, I bumped into another friend, Deb, who lived not far from Aidy. She asked with a cheeky smile: 'You see me the other morning?' I was not too sure what she was talking about until she revealed that just after having had a morning shower, she had heard me flying around so had raced out onto the lawn in her dressing gown 'flashing at me'. Unfortunately I was not flying that day but Ray Patchett, who was spraying grapes next door was, and saw a good display. She could be forgiven — both planes look and sound similar.

The few difficult times of flying have been well and truly compensated for by some of the most exhilarating and fulfilling days of my veterinary career. Just a few minutes after finishing a job and getting back to the plane, I'm over the range and into the next valley. On the way I might pass a friend mustering on a farm track in his Toyota. Wild goats scatter for cover, a sow with her litter trots on, a couple of deer look up. I land and finish the next job and am back in the plane for another little thrill before the final job of the day, knowing that if I was driving I would still be on the way to the second job.

There are certain features perhaps rather unique to Marlborough. It is a land of numerous mountain ranges and valleys but without exception no interlinking roads between them. We cannot drive up one valley and cross over and come back down another. To the south and east, we visit clients along the east coast as far south as the Clarence River, two large stations — Bluff and Muzzle stations — in the Clarence Valley, and a number in the Awatere Valley, with Molesworth Station the furthest south, extending as far as Hanmer. To go from one valley to the next requires driving all the way back to Seddon, which lies over the Weld Pass, 20 kilometres south of Blenheim. Similarly from Blenheim we have the Waihopai and Avon Valleys, Wairau Valley which extends to the Nelson Lakes, and to the northwest, Havelock and Rai Valley. Getting between these valleys requires driving back to Renwick — 10 kilometres to the west of Blenheim.

And then of course we have the Marlborough Sounds. As much as we enjoy visiting Sounds properties, getting there involves hours of driving and possibly some time on a boat. So when driving we try and organise a full day in one valley, or two at most, to make things more efficient and to save on mileage charges to farmers. Farm locality is of course not too much of a problem when flying, and it is not uncommon for me to visit four or five properties in two or three different valleys in one day; two to four hours' driving in a day versus an hour by air.

There have been so many interesting flights. I have been an air ambulance to man and beast on more than one occasion. One of my messier jobs was returning a huntaway pup to Graham Black, a delightful, generous and very experienced merino farmer in the Awatere Valley. The pup had been in the clinic for several days with a disease often fatal to dogs, parvovirus. Parvovirus causes severe enteritis, intestinal inflammation, the main symptoms being constant vomiting and diarrhoea, and even when aggressive early treatment is initiated, is often fatal.

This pup had apparently fully recovered and was ready to go home. Graham was not going to be in town for several days and as I was flying to do a job on his property, I was asked to take the dog with me. I soon found out that he had not recovered fully. While driving from the clinic to the plane at Omaka, he proceeded to vomit through his travel cage onto the back seat of my car. Parvovirus vomit has a distinctive, cloying smell and the scent lingered long after the incident. Swearing and cursing at the poor little vomiting dog, I cleaned up the car as best I could at the hangar and then loaded the plane with my gear and the pup and headed off up the Awatere Valley. Worse than the smell of parvo vomit is parvo diarrhoea. Ten minutes into the flight I again became aware of a distinct parvo smell. Sure enough, looking into the back I could see the poor little miserable pup squirting very watery, blood-stained bowel content all over the equipment and the luggage compartment of the Colt. There was nothing I could do but fly on. Now I also had a plane with a near permanent parvo smell.

One day I had several jobs in the Sounds when later in the afternoon I was presented with an old huntaway that had been trampled by a cow that morning. He was in severe respiratory distress. There was an obvious broken rib or two and a pneumothorax — a condition where air has escaped from the lungs into the chest cavity and the lungs collapsed. I aspirated some air from the chest, which certainly helped but more work needed to be done at the clinic — more than I could do on the airstrip in the Sounds. He was a quiet old dog and seemed quite content to sit behind my seat in the Colt. Well, he was until we were over Picton. It was then that he decided it was time to bail out. It is not much fun flying with a panicking respiratory-distressed dog clawing at the window, the back of your neck, the seat, the roof, while barking and growling. In fact, just trying his best to wreck you and the plane and get out. I had to fly with one hand, and try and hold him down with the other. Eventually his need for oxygen overcame all else and he collapsed. On landing I managed to drag the semi-conscious dog onto the runway and aspirate more air from his chest. He survived but bits of the interior of the plane didn't.

On a visit to Molesworth Station one morning to do several jobs on a few horses, the house cow, and vaccinate some dogs, I noticed Don Reid, the manager, was nursing his arm a bit. Now Don is one of those typical tough high country people who is often more concerned about his animals than himself and didn't say too much, other than he had a bit of a sore elbow after a mare had clouted it when he was shoeing it a couple of days earlier. However, the elbow was not working too well and when I finally encouraged him to let me have a look, it was obvious that something was broken. So he flew back to Blenheim with me and went to the hospital to get his arm looked at and I continued into the Sounds. When I returned from the Sounds, there he was at Omaka, the local aerodrome, with his arm in a cast and sling. He needed to get back home, so I then flew him home to Molesworth. Two flights to the Molesworth and one into the Sounds where we had to land at a couple of challenging strips may have only been a little over four hours' flying but it was still a big day for me.

One thing I soon learnt was that it was important to have a 'check list' of the day's requirements. This is usually done the day before flying. It is important for two very good reasons.

Firstly, with a check list I could tick off all requirements for the day including simple things like boots and overalls as they were loaded into the plane. Once that was done I could give full attention to the very important pre-flight check of the plane. Being distracted by thoughts of what you might have forgotten while doing the plane check and missing something could have nasty consequences. The other reason was that running out of important drugs, such as tuberculin for TB testing, which has happened two hours' flying away, interrupts the day somewhat when you have to fly back to town and collect more. This has happened, as has finding on arrival at one property that I was going to have to manually pregnancy test 350 cows without gloves or lubricant. The arm hairs get a fair pummelling when that happens. So the check list is very important.

Passengers can actually be an issue. When it is a beautiful day, the strips are not too demanding, and your passenger enjoys flying, then it's a thrill to have someone with you to enjoy what you are doing and seeing. However, when the weather is a little inclement, or the strips are a challenge, or they are not enjoying it, then passengers just become another responsibility and stress factor. I am now far more hesitant about agreeing to take passengers with me, especially in the Pawnee where the passenger is fairly crammed in the dickie seat, which is behind the engine and in front of the hopper. The pop-up canopy used when I have a passenger alters the view for the pilot and also seems to have some influence on the aerodynamics of the plane.

Some passengers I have not enjoyed. I remember a German vet student who came with me to some remote magnificent areas of the province, but all he could say when I asked him if he enjoyed what he saw was 'Ja'. I had done the flight many times before and as usual was buzzing from the trip and he couldn't demonstrate even the slightest bit of enthusiasm. Another final year vet student, an American girl who spent two months staying at our home, complained about everything including the weather, the food, and when she came on a flight, my landings. She only had one flight with me!

However many, especially some of the locals, who have flown with me have come away on a high, buzzing from the experience. They have seen country for the first time from a different aspect — country they have lived relatively close to all their lives, and never really appreciated.

Once we had a South African vet staying with us. He lived next to the Kruger National Park and knew all about spectacular sights. He spent a day with me when I flew into the Clarence and Awatere Valleys. It was a calm early spring day and when we flew between the two valleys, I took him up the snow-covered gullies and ridges of Mt Alarm and then along the ridge and around the summit of Mt Tapuae-o-Uenuku. It was a magnificent sight and the whole way I got this one-word running commentary: 'Beautiful, beautiful.' That man has become a friend for life.

A delightful Danish veterinary student, Tina, who ended up living with my family for over two months and with whom we still keep in regular touch, came flying with me into the Sounds one day. However, before we went there our first stop was at Rainbow Station, at the head of the Wairau Valley. There is a good top-dressing strip there, running parallel to the main road, but this day the grass was long and it was hard to see where the actual strip was. I definitely missed it and touched down a couple of metres to one side where the ground was very rough. The Pawnee immediately became airborne after hitting a rise and then went through several severe rocking motions when we touched down again as one wheel then the other went into a hollow as we careered up the paddock alongside the strip. It was a very rough landing and thankfully we were in the Pawnee and not some more fragile machine. When I climbed out, shaking a little, and let Tina out she had this enormous grin on her face.

'That was so exciting,' she said. 'I love this coming to the ground bit at the end best of all. Oh Pete, that was sooo ... much fun.'

By the end of the day she appreciated that not all my landings were quite so exciting.

It is often at the end of the day when flying comes into its own and can't be surpassed. I have half an hour's work left and then know I will be strapped into the Pawnee and cruising home, not having to think about the long drive back to town into the night on narrow, winding, dusty roads. The sun has gone down and there is a red glow in the sky to the west, there is not a breath of wind and all is calm. A trustworthy 1940s technology motor throbs away in front of me and I am at peace. In half an hour I am skimming over vineyards to land on our strip beside home. George or Caroline, if at home, will have heard me but not before our two terriers. By the time I have landed, the hangar door is open and I can taxi straight in. The hopper is emptied and materials are already in the back of the ute. I walk a few paces to the house to be greeted by a relieved Chick and a tumbler of Laphroaig or Highland Park. Telephone messages and tomorrow's arrangements can wait until after dinner. Life is sweet.

PUNCTUALITY — PJ

Vets are always late. That is, country vets are always late. In my more recent capacity as a companion animal vet, I have a phobic fear of keeping people waiting, unlike another of my colleagues who in all other respects I admire enormously.

Stuart is a fantastic vet and a lovely man, but on time? Never. If a meeting is due to start at midday, 12.20 is fine for Stu, while I gnash my teeth in silent fury. If there are two people waiting for me in the waiting room, I have failed my clients. Four is no problem for Stuart, even though they all have scheduled times. He should be called Teflon Stu. It never sticks to him. People who have been angrily checking their watches for 40 minutes come out of their consultation with Stuart smiling happily and thinking of the letter of appreciation they are going to send him. He's just so thoroughly nice that he gets away with it.

But I have this old-fashioned belief that as I don't like being kept waiting, neither should I make my own clients wait for me.

That is in the controlled environment of the clinic. We have receptionists, we have nurses, we have cages to put dogs and cats in if their consultation reveals the need for X-rays, or minor surgery, or an anaesthetic to check a ligament or a fracture.

On farm calls, however, it's very different, particularly in extensive areas such as Marlborough. It can be 20 to 50 minutes from one farm to the next on winding shingle roads.

There is the 'while you're here' syndrome with which all country vets are familiar. 'Oh, while you're here, the daughter's horse is lame', or 'there's a ram with a foot abscess', or 'one of the calves has a bulge under its belly'.

These things may add anywhere from five minutes to two hours to your call.

Or while you're pregnancy testing 200 cows, 100 break out of the yards and have to be rounded up. Another hour gone. We're always late, and farmers, bless their souls, are mostly understanding and say nowt.

We don't have good cell-phone coverage in some of Marlborough's valleys either (and for a long time there was no such thing), so it isn't always possible to ring ahead to let them know. In fact, it is my belief that unless farmers have the first call of the day, they expect their vets to be late, and plan accordingly.

But one morning, at the very beginning of my career, when I was yet a student, and cell phones were as unlikely as The Second Coming, Peter Anderson was heading to see a fairly local dairy farmer, only 10 minutes from town. All this land is now in grapes, but at that time there were a few smallish town supply dairy farms scattered about the Wairau Plain, all close to Blenheim. They were a small but interesting and significant part of our vet practice.

Danny Garfield had 100 cows, three young children and a mortgage. He was a nice man, but a bit chaotic. Things were always going wrong. If it wasn't a strong electric current leaking into the cups of the milking machine and upsetting the cows, it was a damaged seal in the supply line to the milk tank.

There was gear everywhere: old tractors, and various ground-tilling implements from days gone by rusting under a macrocarpa hedge or gathering weeds in the muddle of small paddocks near the house. Fences were ragged and not always stock proof, and some of the gates would swing reasonably well when opened, or when you untwisted the piece of wire keeping them shut.

There always seemed to be a lot of washing on the line and Danny always seemed to be three steps behind where he wished he was.

Pete and I headed out to see him at 8.30 this spring morning. As we turned off the road onto his drive, I could see hurried activity ahead. Arms were waving, two dogs were skulking 200 metres away, and 30 or 40 calves were kicking up their heels in what looked suspiciously like the vegetable garden. A milk tanker was parked beside the shed, the driver pacing anxiously. His schedule was tight; the factory didn't like waiting for the day's milk. A modern tractor lay at a funny angle, trailer and calf crate attached, in the paddock beside the milking shed.

As we came closer, we could see the arms belonged to Danny. Normally an equable man, he stopped for only a second, then rushed past. I could clearly hear the words he spat out as he raced by, his oversized gumboots tripping him in the long grass.

'What a bloody day! The calves have got out, the pump's broken down, the tractor's stuck, the tanker's here and waiting, and now the bloody vet's on time!'

Sometimes it's best to say nothing.

AT THE ZOO — PA

In 1982 the Marlborough Zoological Gardens opened after five years of fund-raising, bureaucratic obstacles and ridiculous building requirements. It seemed certain members of the local catchment board and their associates had had other plans for the chosen site, on low-lying land near the Wairau River, a short distance from Renwick. The Marlborough Zoological Society's own plan for an exotic animal park modelled after Orana Park in Christchurch was in the way.

Nevertheless, the enthusiasts, largely volunteer, persevered and the facilities were finally built and ready for their first residents.

One of the problems with stocking a wildlife park is that you tend to acquire, often at considerable expense, other people's castoffs. Zoos can find surplus animals of some species, black buck, peccaries and even lions, for example, problematic to dispose of, so these were not hard to pick up. However, with others it seemed we were an outlet for the misfits.

Olly the Ostrich was a sexual deviant who spent his whole life trying to mate anything else with two legs, including visitors observing him through the fence. If we had been able to source a mate for him, he may have improved but unfortunately this was not possible at the time.

A large dominant male grey kangaroo, Boomer, was also a bit of an embarrassment. He spent most of his day showing off an incredibly impressive erection and masturbating on all the smaller pine trees that dotted his enclosure. This sort of behaviour is difficult to curb. He also urinated through the netting around his enclosure at people as they marvelled at his antics.

We also tended to acquire a number of older animals that were naturally not as attractive as younger, fitter animals for displaying at zoos. As a result we had to deal with a few degenerative conditions including kidney failure in a lion, kidney stones in otters and teeth problems in a tiger.

Diagnosing when you are faced with a sick animal in a wildlife park is not without its problems. Firstly it is impossible to have some sort of restraining device in every enclosure and even if we did, getting them into one was always difficult. Secondly, most zoo animals are difficult or very dangerous to handle, and thirdly any restraining or handling often exacerbated the situation and you ended up with an even sicker animal. In a number of cases we had to resort to tranquillising sick animals, and heavily in the case of the lions and tigers, to examine them. The dart gun was very useful for this. However, a tranquillised animal, while allowing easy collection of blood or other samples, does not behave normally or respond much to stimuli, which complicated accurate diagnosis. Equally, making a diagnosis on a stressed-out, panicking animal is not easy either.

While blood tests might help, the results don't come back for a day or two. Therefore you often opt for on-the-spot diagnoses while the animal is restrained. If you wait, you may have missed your only opportunity to get close enough to treat it.

We usually used a rather shotgun approach to treatment as we needed to cover all fields. Restraining the animal for daily injections was out of the question, while medication in the feed was invariably unsuccessful. Medicating the feed might mean treating all other animals in the enclosure, which could be very expensive and usually didn't work because sick animals invariably did not eat.

However, all the animals were very well cared for and fed and generally in good health. Good programmes were in place to prevent outbreaks of parasitism and those diseases preventable by vaccinating. Some of the diseases we had to deal with were ones that little could be done about. This included two untreatable viral diseases — malignant catarrh fever (MCF) and bovine viral diarrhoea (BVD). These two viruses really took out our water buffalo and bison populations and were quite a tragedy for the park. Prevention by vaccination was not possible at that time.

Once, over a period of a few months, we had to deal with a series of sudden traumatic deaths of several animals including two Barbary sheep, a chamois and a fallow deer. All had been badly gored and we couldn't figure it out until early one morning a Himalayan tahr was observed making his way back to his enclosure via the top of deer fence posts — a serial killer with incredible agility and a good head for heights.

Despite keeping potentially dangerous animals, there was never a major breakout, although we came close once when the head keeper failed to lock a door in the lion enclosure. PJ tells the story:

I didn't do much work at the wildlife park. Pete A had been their vet from the beginning, and had done all the exciting things such as vasectomising the tiger in Christchurch before it came to

Marlborough. One day, however, I did get my share of the thrills.

It was not long after PA and I had set up on our own. I was alone in our little clinic on Main Street when the phone rang. It was Murray Robers, the manager of the park. His voice was tremulous.

'Can you come quickly? The tiger is out! Bring the dart gun.'

That's quite a dramatic start to a call-out, one that not too many vets will have faced. My mind was racing as I unlocked the safe and retrieved the dart gun, a handful of darts and a bottle of Fentaz, a lethal mixture of fentanyl and azaperone. I didn't waste much time jumping into my little Datsun Sunny and tearing off westward to Renwick. At Springlands, on the outskirts of Blenheim, I turned left, then right onto Lakings Road, to my house. I had a .243 calibre rifle, barely enough to stop a tiger, but if I got a clean headshot it might.

The problem with the dart gun was two-fold: I would have to get very close to be accurate and effective, not a pleasant thought; and even if I got a clean contact it would take 15 minutes to knock him out. He could eat a few residents and a vet in that time.

I didn't like my chances, so the rifle was going to be the better option. I put a packet of 105-grain ammunition on the seat and hurried towards Renwick again. My mind was running amok. How would I find it? Was it already terrorising the good citizens of Renwick, maybe gnawing on the local butcher right now?

A vision came into my mind. For many years I hunted deer, chamois, tahr, and wapiti all over the South Island. I pictured myself getting a clean headshot, and could see the picture on the front page of the *Marlborough Express* of the great hunter, one foot on the dead tiger's head, rifle resting butt down on the shoulder. The headline would read VET SAVES RENWICK. With the photo it would take the entire front page.

The thought rapidly dissipated as I got nearer. I was very

VET SAVES RENWICK !

nervous as I turned in to the road where the park was, cautiously watching for bristling whiskers or a lashing striped tail. I reached the office. Murray was waiting. He looked shocked.

'He went back in,' he croaked. He was shaking, and looked very, very relieved.

The story went like this. It was in fact one of the lions, not the tiger, who had escaped. Murray was so shocked at the time that 'tiger' came out instead of 'lion'.

There were double gates into the lion cage, and a set procedure to follow when entering and leaving, for feeding or any other reason. The keeper would go through the first door, then shut it behind himself, so he was in a secure separate area between the gates. Then, carefully making sure the animals weren't too close, he would open the inner door, chuck the feed in, shut that one, then open the first door again to go and get more food. On this occasion he had broken the inviolable rule. He'd left the inner gate open as he went back for more food, believing the lion was out of the way and concentrating on the meat he'd just thrown it. When he turned around with the extra feed, the hungry and curious lion was walking through the gate towards him.

He bolted into the outer enclosure, which was surrounded by a deer fence, and shot out of that via a small gate. The lion was secured only by a two-metre deer fence, an easy leap for an adult big cat. A woolly romney hogget lived in the enclosure. The lion grabbed it, played with it like a cat with a mouse for a few minutes, then tired of the game and strolled back into its cage. The hogget was unharmed but had a tale to tell her many grandchildren, although I doubt any believed her.

It was a near thing, and Murray knew it. I was pretty damned relieved myself, but I always had just a small hankering wistfulness about the episode. The photo and the headline would have been great to show *my* grandchildren.

(*PA continues*...) Despite the problems the park did work. Animals seemed contented and those that could bred well. Although the area started off bare and stark, it was soon developing nicely with many trees and gardens planted and growing well. It was becoming aesthetically pleasing. Unfortunately it struggled financially although desperate fund-raising activities by service clubs such as The Blenheim Round Table helped keep it afloat. The final straw was in July 1983 when Blenheim had a major flood. Most of the farmyard animals and some water buffalo drowned and though the otters survived, for some reason they died soon after. The peccaries swam in their enclosure for hours but did survive.

PJ and I managed to make our way to the park at the peak of the flood and spent a full day there wading between enclosures and shepherding the animals to the highest ground. Here the herbivores had to be mixed. However, the floods did produce some amazing scenes of camaraderie among the animals. In a badly flooded area a water buffalo, antelope, kangaroo, chamois and tahr sought refuge by crowding together on a small mound of high ground.

Nine weeks of rebuilding and repair work were required before the park could be opened again. However, this was a significant cost and the park never fully recovered financially. We had to make a decision on whether to close down or rebuild. Eventually a loan to rebuild was taken out but this finally proved too much to repay in that period of high inflation and interest rates. The number of visitors was just not sufficient to maintain the park and its outgoings. In spite of help from many sources, it always struggled financially and finally the decision to close was made in 1988.

THE TWO RONNIES — PJ

Embryo transfer. The very term still makes me prick my ears and sharpen my senses. It epitomised state-of-the-art technology and was something which we had quite a bit to do with in the 1980s and even into the early 1990s.

Embryo transfer in cattle, sheep, goats and deer involves a complex programme of treating female animals with various sex hormones to make them produce multiple eggs (or ova) during the breeding season. The female is then mated with a bull, ram, buck or stag, and as males have very large numbers of sperm, one hopes there will be multiple fertilised embryos.

These embryos have to be harvested by flushing them from the uterus of the female at about one week post-mating, before the embryos have permanently implanted into the wall of the uterus.

The harvested embryos are then implanted, usually on the same day, into numerous other females of the same species, whose fertility cycle has been coordinated with the original, or donor, female. This ensures that the implanted embryos are receiving the correct hormones for their stage of life. It's quite complex, yet in the 1980s many New Zealand vets joined the boom of the goat world, and later the deer world, in performing embryo transfer or ET.

In cattle, the flushing and implanting is comparatively simple, as the vet can palpate the cow's uterus with a hand in her rectum. The cow doesn't need an anaesthetic or surgery. But with goats, sheep and deer, much smaller animals, it all has to be done surgically, and usually in a purpose-built surgery on the farm. It demands a high skill level and much attention to detail.

When we were doing goats, we would have to get a locum vet and nurse into the clinic for a month in April, and adjust everything else we did to fit around ET. It was highly exciting from a professional point of view, and pretty damned nerve-wracking too. There was a lot of money at stake.

Enter the two Ronnies.

Ronnie A was one of the first deer farmers in Marlborough. Big, bluff, scary, he bought whisky by the case, sold a lot of stags around New Zealand and by his own reckoning had the best stags in the country. He wanted to do embryo transfer from his top eight hinds to speed up the production of high-quality stock.

Ronnie B was a real go-getter. He'd had a go at everything from possum trapping for fur to gold mining, from the mussel industry to the grape industry. He had a small deer farm with one outstanding hind.

The two Ronnies, hard men if ever there were, formed a sort of alliance, and approached Anderson and Jerram to do some ET for them. Ronnie A wanted eight hinds done, and they would bring Ronnie B's one hind to that farm to programme her with hormones.

We settled on a professional fee, set up the programme, and away we went.

On the big day, the first of two, we carefully anaesthetised the first hind, one of Ronnie A's. After clipping and cleaning her abdomen, and scrubbing up fully, I opened her up with a small slit midline. I found the uterus, made a tiny incision, and passed the Foley catheter, a tube with an outer balloon, into the uterus. I inflated the balloon, then as PA passed me a sterile syringe full of the flushing liquid, I carefully catheterised the fallopian tubes. I squeezed the syringe, and fluid flowed through the fallopian tube and into the uterus. As the pressure came on, the fluid, hopefully having picked up the embryos floating in the uterus, would flow into the catheter and out the other end where PA had a collecting dish. Each hind has two flushes, one for each horn of the uterus, and each flush is a moment of great tension. We're dealing with live tissue, easily ruptured and ruined forever, and we want to get these embryos for our client. With each flush we feel like Dan Carter taking the winning kick in the World Cup final.

After we've flushed, PA takes the collection dish to a microscope at his bench and searches the liquid for the tiny embryos. As he finds them, he carefully sucks them up and deposits them into another smaller dish, then stores them in a large incubator, the size of a commercial refrigerator, behind him. This keeps them at body temperature until we implant them.

You can cut the air with a knife as the two Ronnies, my nurse assistant, and I wait for PA to give his verdict. I stitch the hind's belly up, give her a shot of antibiotic, and the men carry her out to the recovery room.

'Two,' PA announces. We have harvested just two embryos.

That's disappointing. We'd hoped for at least six or eight. Ronnie A isn't disconsolate, however. 'There'll be more in the next ones.'

He's an optimist, the cup is always half full. We carry on with the next three hinds.

'Eight.' The next one, jubilation.

'Nothing.' Shit.

'Six.' The fourth one, complacent smile.

From four hinds we have 16 embryos. It's not brilliant, but it's better than nothing.

We spend the rest of the day implanting those into the eight recipient hinds. I use a laparoscope, which means we can implant the anaesthetised recipient deer without full surgery.

At the end of the day, Ronnie A is still cheerful. His day hasn't been overly successful, but not a flop. He has three more hinds to flush. Ronnie B has one hind to flush. We'll do her tomorrow.

The next day is crisp and clear. A light frost tinges the Wairau Plain, and the green bushy hills to the north are stark and clear against the clear autumn sky. We are at the deer shed surgery by 8am, ready to go.

We flush the next hind. 'Ten,' calls PA. A good result and Ronnie A is full of enthusiasm. 'Nought.' The next one, Ronnie isn't so happy.

'Four.' Ronnie A's final hind.

Thirty embryos from seven hinds. OK but still a little disappointing. It is Ronnie B's turn.

We flush his hind, a strapping red deer with ear tag Yellow 64. It's a blinder.

'Eighteen, bloody ripper,' calls PA quietly from his microscope.

We're delighted, but our pleasure is nothing compared with Ronnie B's. He's in seventh heaven. His chest puffs out and he struts around the shed, especially when he comes close to Ronnie A.

'You'd have thought he'd fathered the bloody things himself,' I muttered to PA.

I was feeling for Ronnie A, who had set the whole programme up, had put up the majority of the hinds and therefore carried the risk. He was looking pretty uncomfortable. A funny thing, competition between strong men.

The strutting didn't stop either.

'Eighteen from one hind. I'll tell you what,' boomed Ronnie B, 'bloody good hind that.'

In the end it became a bit unbearable. I don't remember whose idea it was but we hatched a plot.

Peter A made up a fresh collection dish, put water in it, nothing else, and wrote with indelible pen in large letters 'Yellow 64, 18 BIG EMBRYOS'. It contained none, but it looked as though it did — embryos are microscopic. He put the dish into the incubator behind where he sat. It was lunchtime; we would implant the whole 32 embryos, 14 of Ronnie A's and 18 of Ronnie B's that afternoon.

As the two Ronnies waited, one with chest out, one trying to avoid his mate, I called to Ronnie B: 'Would you like to have a look at these embryos?'

'Would I what! Where are they?' He began to strut towards PA, seated at his microscope.

'Careful,' I warned, 'these things are delicate. You don't want to bump PA. You could lose the lot.' Only slightly chastened, he waited impatiently as I led him into the rough laboratory.

'Pete, Ronnie B wants to look at his eighteen embryos.' I said it carefully as if PA might not want to upset things. 'OK,' said PA. He carefully put the top on the dish of real embryos he was looking at, opened the door of the incubator behind him, and placed the dish on a rack inside. Then just as carefully, he brought out the dish he'd marked earlier.

Ever so carefully he placed the bogus dish on the microscope stage. He took off the clear lid.

'Need to get a clear look at these.' An authoritative Ronnie B pushed forward.

'Careful,' said PA. 'Don't bump me.' He peered down the microscope.

'These are just the best embryos you'd see,' he enthused. 'Big buggers. Would you like a look?'

Ronnie B nodded eagerly, straining at the leash. PA started to get off the high stool he sat on but as he moved, he appeared to have a clumsy accident. His hand brushed the dish on the microscope. It fell off the microscope stage, landing upside down on the wooden bench. The apparently precious fluid, supposedly full of embryos, spread all over the bench and began to dribble over the edge onto the floor.

Stunned, Ronnie B could only croak: 'Is that it?'

Pete A looked up wide-eyed. He nodded. He couldn't say anything.

'Well, can't you suck them up, fast, now?,' yelled Ronnie.

With one bare hand cupped under the bench, Pete A used the other one to sweep some of the spilt fluid into the cupped one, seemingly trying to catch the microscopic organisms with his bare hands.

It was too much. He caught my eye and we both exploded into gut-wrenching laughter.

'It's OK, Ronnie,' said PA. 'We're only having you on. The real ones are still in there.' He pointed to the incubator.

'You bastards,' Ronnie B stormed out. Ronnie A, in on the story, felt a lot better, and eventually Ronnie B could laugh about it too. But he did take six months to pay the bill.

I think all but one of the recipient hinds held at least one embryo and fawned successfully that spring. But I don't think Ronnie B ever did ET again. There's only so much a man can take.

THE OTHER SIDE — PJ

Homosexuality is not a word that sits comfortably with many people. It tends to be pronounced very carefully by newsreaders and social workers, with very clear enunciation and a look in the eye that proclaims, 'There, I've said it.'

In the animal world, homosexuality happens on a regular basis and I'm sure it passes without comment from the rest of the animals. In humans it tends to be more covert, and although accepted and tolerated by a majority of people now, our Victorian-age ethics still apply to some extent and there is still a degree of antipathy towards the idea.

I am not homosexual, and neither is my business partner of nearly 30 years, Peter Anderson. But at least one person may not be so sure.

In my early days at the Graham Veterinary Club, the general populace was emerging from the frugality of post World War II, but only just. People were not, for example, prepared to spend much money on their pets. Now, all is different. A broken leg will be mended for $1000 or even $3000 and pet owners will, more often than not, be prepared, if not happy, to pay for their loved pets. But not then. In 1979, $11 for a consultation and prescription was a lot of money to spend on your cat. As a consequence, many pet owners would ring or turn up at the front counter seeking free advice, or in many cases, prescription drugs to take home and treat their animals. 'A consultation? Eleven dollars? No way. I know what's wrong, just give me the drugs,' was an attitude if not prevalent, then certainly common.

This could create a problem for young vets. Hadn't we been taught the sanctity of prescription drugs, and the importance of a thorough clinical examination before prescribing? Well yes, but the older vets and merchandise manager had been dishing out drugs for years, and as a newcomer you had to be very brave to stick your head up too far to oppose this policy.

Yet I tried, and I always disliked the idea of dishing out a bottle of Albipen tablets to a cat breeder who lived 50 kilometres away and therefore needed them 'on hand', or six bottles of Penstrep injectable to a deer farmer who may have needed it from time to time. So I got into a few discussions at the counter (and so did all the other vets) with some clients who I still think were pretty demanding. There were one or two who kept coming back and back, always for free advice, sometimes even after getting the drugs.

It got so bad that we kept a list of the worst offenders and whenever one of these unfortunates would turn up, there would be a scramble among any vets in the office to be the first to disappear out the back to find something which needed doing urgently. If you were last out then you were stuck with the difficult client.

Some of these people knew a captive audience when they saw one and would just not let go. And gradually, I couldn't say who started it, the other vets, those who had escaped, began the practice of doing anything to distract the victim vet and make him laugh. All sorts of tricks were used and it goes beyond the delicacy of this tome to describe most of them, but those I can mention included funny faces, the occasional show of underwear, and, after a time, a sly pinch on the backside as one walked past the vet at the counter.

If you were the victim, some of these tricks were very hard to resist and I'm sure I offended a few clients with sudden, odd and inappropriate squeals and snorts of laughter as they described their pet's ailments to me. But I tried very hard not to succumb to the offenders, my associates.

One morning, Pete Anderson got caught. My memory fails to place the client across the counter, but she was one of the real heavies. She had PA in her grasp and was going to squeeze every last ounce of information from him, for free. Now, Pete is a very kind and tolerant man, much more so than I, yet even he was starting to shift uncomfortably on his feet, glance at the clock on the wall, and say he had something to do. No way. She wasn't finished yet.

I couldn't resist it. I moved past Pete's back to the filing cabinet, and gave his bum a good squeeze as I went. I found the file I didn't want or need, and as I passed behind him again, gave him another, this one more prolonged, almost, dare I say it, a caress. And just at that moment I became aware that the door at the back of the office had opened while I was going past Pete the first time and hadn't been closed.

With my hand on PA's arse, I looked behind me to the open door. Standing in the doorway, wide-eyed, stunned, was Mrs Gaylene Twyford from Renwick, long a cat breeder. She'd watched me on both passes as she came through the storeroom into the back of the office.

For some reason Gaylene never really wanted to see me again when she brought her cats in. The old dear is dead now but I'm sure she went to her grave convinced that those two Peters at the Vet Club were a couple of homos.

A STINT IN KOSOVO — PA

In July 2001, not long after the conflict in Yugoslavia, I took on a job with the FAO, the Food and Agriculture section of the United Nations, in Kosovo. It came about because Ron Jackson, a New Zealand vet and epidemiologist who travelled the world visiting trouble spots was looking for someone who might be interested in working there.

At the time of my arrival, a 28,000-strong NATO-led security force involving 35 nations patrolled Kosovo. NATO had become involved after the Kosovo Liberation Army — Albanian revolutionaries — had risen up against Slobodan Milosevic and his Serbian regime, who had been in power since the 1980s. Albanians dominated the population but were treated like second-class citizens. The Serbs retaliated and the conflict became bloody so NATO took control. Those Serbs remaining in Kosovo were subjected to revenge attacks and most lived in 'enclaves'. When visiting them, we had to go via guard posts.

Disintegration of the Serbian leadership had left a policy

void relating to animal health services. No one knew what to do, no one knew what diseases were important and there were no defined responsibilities for the private and public sectors. Ron was pretty well in charge of defining the situation and determining what was required. One thing he felt was needed was someone to get local vets thinking about herd and flock health programmes. So I responded to his request for a vet with suitable experience in this line of work to help.

Agriculture is important for Kosovo, which has a population of two million and is one of the poorer regions in Europe. Outside the main towns, most of these people live in villages comprising perhaps 80 houses with 30-40 of the houses owning a cow or two. During the crisis the cows were either stolen or shot and eaten by the Serbs, so the returning Albanians had no cows — vitally important to them for milk, yogurt and cheese, which make up a significant part of their diet. To overcome this crisis the United Nations gathered up 2500 in-calf Simmental and Swiss Brown heifers, mainly from Austria and Germany, and distributed these to farmers in December 2000 — usually one cow per family. One of the conditions of receiving a cow was that any heifer calf born had to be given back for redistribution and the cow had to be impregnated for the next redistribution. But there were lots of problems with getting these cows back in calf.

Historically the main method of impregnation was by artificial insemination and as a result there were not many bulls around. Unfortunately the critical timing for insemination to take place was invariably missed. Often telephones did not work, the vet might not have access to a car, or the owner missed seeing that the cow was on heat. The big imported heifers, housed for 90 per cent of the day, did not show the typical oestrus behaviour of the small indigenous cow the farmers were used to. To top it off many of the cow owners could not, forgive the pun, give a 'damn'. Most had other jobs and all were trying to rebuild their lives and their houses. Getting the cow back in calf was low on the priority list. One day while I was there the FAO boss rang from Rome to see how things were going. I don't think he was impressed when I told him we didn't want any more semen from Europe. All we wanted was lots of randy little bulls — Jersey bulls from New Zealand would be ideal.

I was based in Pristina and living at the Park Hotel. It certainly wasn't the Park Royal. In fact it used to be a brothel in the days when the Serbs were in control but unfortunately there was no sign of the previous occupant of my room. The walls were a shocking purple, the water — when it ran — was cold, power was only sometimes on, and sleep was difficult. Very early every morning I would be rudely awoken by calls to prayer from a tone-deaf muezzin shouting through a megaphone on top of a minaret outside my window.

I would walk to the FAO office each morning and then head out with the driver and an Albanian vet, who acted as interpreter, to 'vet stations' around the country. Here we would often spend a good part of the day discussing issues with vets and vet technicians, perhaps visit a few crook animals on farms, and generally try to change the world. It was not an easy mission. Firstly there was a language barrier and difficulties with interpreters. I found talking using an interpreter very tiring and sometimes quite a challenge, not helped by the fact there were always people coming and going during these meetings. Farmers would often charge in and jabber away with the vet, who then leaped up and disappeared for 10 minutes. Sometimes the vet also disappeared to go and do a bit of praying. When he eventually returned, you started up again. Then someone would bring in coffee. This stuff was strong as hell, thick and sweet and not too bad. Once you had had a couple of these you didn't need to eat much for the rest of the day. It was also probably one of the reasons that I didn't sleep well the whole time I was there.

Semi-wild dogs, many apparently with rabies, were common in the city. After dark, these dogs would appear and congregate around the overflowing rubbish skips parked on every second corner, fighting for the best scraps off and on throughout the night. Then as dawn approached they went and holed up somewhere and the crows took over. They made quite a din, as did the mosquitoes, which seemed to enjoy a bit of Kiwi blood. Then the tuneless singing from the minaret eventually forced me to give up all hope of sleep. I could understand why there was tension in the country.

The first few weeks in Kosovo were spent helping local vets learn a few basics, such as pregnancy testing cows and getting them to think about preventative medicine. They were very good at attending to sick animals or calving cows but the bulk of their work revolved around treating 'downer cows' or those with mastitis, and removing retained foetal membranes. Many of the health problems in cows suggested a selenium deficiency, but it was not possible to prove this while I was there because there were no animal health laboratories. Later on some bloods that Ron Jackson had collected for other tests were analysed in Britain and this confirmed very low seleniums. Something about the communist background meant people never asked why. If there was a problem such as a retained placenta, they knew how to remove it but no one had ever thought to ask why they were getting so many. Their philosophy was, 'This is what it is; this is what you do. End of story.'

The written word was also gospel. One day I visited a relatively modern clinic where a very prominent and respected vet was treating an old horse with what appeared to be chronic parasitism. He was stomach tubing it, which involves gently feeding a plastic hose through the nasal passages and down the oesophagus to the stomach, and then pouring the medicine down the tube. In this case he was using an early type anthelmintic, or wormer. When I suggested he might like to try a newer more effective product, Ivomectin, because we had found it very successful in such cases, he refused to even contemplate it. He kept telling me that it was only for cattle. I kept telling him that it also works well in horses. He got more and more angry and then stomped off and brought out a packet of Ivomec which admittedly did say 'for cattle only'. In his mind if it wasn't written down that it was for horses, then it wasn't for horses. End of story. And no one, least of all a vet from New Zealand, wherever that was, was going to tell him otherwise.

Most cows were locked up in their small barn for most of the day and only let out for a couple of hours of grazing — if they were lucky. Conserved food, mainly hay and meal, was brought to them. As the soil seemed very fertile and grew great lucerne, I wondered why stock were not grazed outside for longer periods. The lack of fencing was probably the main reason. I thought electric fencing would have been very useful but when I finally got one farmer to understand the concept, he proudly told me that my idea wouldn't work — the fence would be stolen.

I think another reason the calves were never let outside was because they didn't know how to control them. I went to one farm where the calf, which was about two months old, was with its mother in a stifling hot, crammed barn with shocking ventilation. It had sore feet and horrible skin lesions and from what I could gather had never been outside. I told the farmer, in fluent Albanian of course, to bring it out of the smelly hovel and give it some fresh air

— which he reluctantly did. The calf, on a very long leash, was so delighted that he ran about skipping and jumping and knocking everyone over, and came right immediately — all he needed was a bit of fresh air, exercise and sunlight.

The Serbs behaved differently to the Albanians and the whole time I was there I never went into an Albanian farmhouse. The Albanian wife, all dressed in black, would usually rush out with coffee after we had finished a job and then vanish. We would sit down in the shade under a tree and quietly drink our thick, black, sweet tumbler of coffee. It was a very male-orientated society.

The few Serbs I met were very different. One day we visited a Serb vet and his wife at their home under some large old plum trees in an enclave. We were invited inside his house, introduced to his wife and family and before we could get into any meaningful discussion had to try his homemade yogurt, and then his homemade cheese and finally his homemade slivovic, a fermented plum alcohol and a potent brew.

However, that was after we had waited for him for some time to return from a call on the other side of the enclave to AI a cow. I expected him to roll up in a Skoda but instead he turned up pushing a squeaky wheelbarrow containing his semen tank. We then sat down in his house and memories of my student days flooded back. It smelt like a student flat, was as untidy as a student flat, and we were all drunk by 11am. By midday we knew everything, had solved all the world's problems, and the four of us —Albanian vet interpreter, driver, Serbian vet and Kiwi vet were exceptionally good buggers. Of course every time we refilled and drained our tumblers we had to leap to our feet, link arms, and give each other a whiskery kiss — right cheek, left cheek, and then right cheek again, and toast something. The Serbian vet sang his national anthem, I did a haka. All good stuff and eventually we staggered out of the house and back to FAO headquarters where I proceeded to tell the project manager, whom everyone seemed suitably terrified of, how to solve the world's problems, including his own.

Before I left the Serb vet, with much ceremony he gave me a bottle of the good stuff — all nicely wrapped up in a plastic bag. So after sorting out the project manager I headed back to the ex-brothel and gave the bottle another wee nudge. I felt I deserved it, because in my opinion it had been a very successful day.

After I had spent a few weeks working with dairy cows and their clients and the dairy vets, I headed south to the pretty town of Prizren. The nicely cobbled, tree-lined streets were only spoiled by the rubbish which lay everywhere. In fact most of Kosovo was covered in rubbish. I spent a couple of weeks in the area looking into how sheep were managed and spent time talking to sheep vets and managers of the flocks.

Sheep are farmed principally for their milk in Kosovo. The indigenous breed, the Sharri, is often crossed with a German breed (Wintemberg), the cross producing a fast-growing lamb. Owners house their sheep at home over the winter but after lambing, the flocks, which are often only a handful of ewes, are driven up to beautiful rolling hill country with natural clover-dominant pastures where they join with other flocks and are managed in mobs of around 120 ewes. Here they are looked after by a team of four or five shepherds for the summer. The shepherds live in very primitive facilities, hand milking the sheep twice a day and because of wild dogs and wolves, yarding them at night. The milk is made into cheese on site and then transported to town by horse once a week. Despite the lack of hygiene and the abundance of flies crawling over all stages of the cheese maturation process, the finished product was delicious.

Kosovo was an interesting experience for me but in many ways quite frustrating. There were a number of diseases that could have been easily controlled, but the lack of enthusiasm of farmers and vets to change could be understood. Farmers were poor as the financial return for their products was generally very low. Bartering between neighbours helped them survive. There was no infrastructure set up to process milk and this was not encouraged or helped by cheap products being dumped into Kosovo from neighbouring countries. There appeared to be a general lack of enthusiasm from local vets to change their ways and improve their services. As one said to me early on in my visit, 'Why prevent? We make our money out of treating.'

As there were 'experts' from all over the world in all areas of society trying to tell them what to do and how to manage their lives, they were becoming, as one vet put it, 'experted out'. There were huge changes taking place and what was once, for the majority, a peasant-type existence ruled by an unpopular Serb minority with curfews every night and controlled by an unforgiving military, was now a free society. Just being able to walk the streets at night with their families was a luxury. There were enough changes taking place without the added stress of trying to make them change their ways of farming or vetting.

As I have mentioned I did find it a challenge to communicate through an interpreter all day but it sometimes had its funny side. One morning we visited a relatively large dairy farm, milking about 60 cows and managed by a woman. This was most unusual. She ran a good operation and I was impressed. At the end of the visit I was, through the interpreter, complimenting her on her set up, how she managed it, the excellent hygiene, how her cows looked and their production, and that she also had very nice breasts. I didn't for one minute think the interpreter would say everything word for word. Well he did. Luckily she didn't appear to be too upset with what I said and I heard later that she had wanted me to revisit her dairy before I left.

My work in Kosovo was meant to be a two-trip mission. Reports from other vets who had worked in the area went to great lengths to justify ongoing visits, but in my opinion our effectiveness was always going to be limited until a milk treatment factory was built and the Kosovo farmers were paid properly for their milk. Then vets might be reimbursed properly, and might be a little more enthusiastic about improving their services. For now they had had enough of experts telling them what to do.

On my debriefing in Rome, I told them not to waste their money and my time. Advisors were only going to be really effective if they, the local Kosovo vets, knew what they wanted. Up until now, they had been so isolated that most didn't appreciate how far behind they really were. They certainly didn't like being told that. Getting a local vet who was well respected by others in Kosovo to gain overseas experience was an idea put forward after I left. This would be far more effective and apparently has since happened.

Needless to say the FAO has not asked me back. However, I wouldn't have missed the experience for anything.

THE WALL OF DEATH — PJ

Although Pete and I were philosophically farmers' vets, we were part of an era where country vets had to do everything. Whether calving a cow in the middle of the night, foaling a mare (always an urgent matter), examining a guinea pig's skin or fixing a dog's broken leg, we did it. Sadly, those days have largely gone. A few old-timers still hang on, but in this era of a population ever ready to complain, and with all the consumer rights to encourage litigation, vets, like all of the professions, are now much more specialised.

Back in the 1980s and 1990s we were James Herriot types — we'd have a go at anything, and without being immodest, I think that we can be reasonably satisfied that we were good small animal vets as well. The economy had turned by then and suddenly there was money to spend on the family dog and cat, something which an earlier generation wouldn't have entertained.

The result was that the small animal side of our business began to boom and we had to keep current in our continuing education in all aspects of small animal medicine and surgery.

Pete A was always a very good soft-tissue surgeon, neat

and tidy and efficient. I was more interested in the mechanics of orthopaedics and later became quite well versed in dog reproduction matters. But we still had to take what came, day and night.

Digressing only a little, we once employed an English vet for three months during the embryo transfer season. Peter Orpin (yes, a third Pete) was a tremendous fellow and a very good vet, and with Bronwen, remains a special friend of ours to this day. We chose him because his CV said he could juggle and eat an apple at the same time! The period that he was with us in the mid-1980s, was just as our economy picked up, yet New Zealanders were still practical, sensible people who knew when things could wait and who didn't like bothering vets after hours unless they had a real emergency. Pete Orpin told us one day that it was not unusual for vets in the UK to be rung at 3am by a client whose cat had diarrhoea. At the time we thought this hugely amusing.

'That will never happen here,' we chuckled

By the late 1990s, it was happening here, and still is. We seem to have an increasingly urban population who are less able to solve problems and who always look to someone else for help. So veterinarians on duty for small animals are just as likely, and in fact in our practice far more likely, to be called out after hours than a large animal vet.

The call could be for all sorts of things.

Kevin was a good chap, young and go-ahead, running his quite large retail and service business, and with the boom in housing just beginning, he was doing all right. He'd married Laurelle, a professional in the performing arts and a little older than him. She'd been attached previously to a slightly dubious character, but was now happily married to Kevin. We used to see one or other of them regularly with their cat or dog. As with most of our clients, we had a nice friendly relationship with them both. But one day Kevin rang and asked for me. His voice was a bit strained.

'Pete, can you come around here with something to tranquillise a wild cat?'

Now, Kevin and Laurelle lived in a nice old two-storeyed house in the centre of Blenheim, so wild cats are a bit unusual there. But there were plenty of wild cats about. We quite often had them brought into the clinic trapped in a possum cage, where it wasn't too hard to get a syringe on a pole through the bars to sedate them.

'Have you got it trapped, Kevin?'

'Well yes, but it's in the downstairs toilet, and I'm not going in there with it.'

It turned out, the cat had been entering Kevin and Laurelle's cat door, harassing their own cat, peeing on the walls and floor, then leaving. Every night.

Laurelle was quite a particular, neat and tidy woman, and Kevin had been given the job of 'doing something about that cat or I won't be coming home'.

Those were her parting words as she headed off three days earlier to hospital in Nelson for minor surgery.

Kevin had heard the familiar wailing from the family cat the night before he rang me and had rushed downstairs and shut the cat door. The wild tom had charged into the lavatory seeking escape and Kevin had slammed the door behind it. But now he had a real dilemma. The cat was really wild, and an angry cat is a very dangerous beast, let alone a wild, angry and trapped one. And Laurelle was due home from hospital the next day.

So he rang the vet.

I packed two pole syringes, a simple push one, and a more

sophisticated spring-loaded one that we used on deer to allow us to get a good volume of drug in very rapidly on a moving target. We'd had lots of practice with the spring syringe, but not on cats. Deer are a bit bigger.

I had to suss out the situation first. I carefully opened the door to the toilet an inch or two. The cat was going wild, doing the wall of death around the walls, which were covered in cat faeces and urine. The smell and the noise were terrific.

Laurelle's beautiful lace curtains were torn to shreds and so was the expensive Liberty patterned wallpaper. I was pretty interested in how Kevin was going to get all this cleaned up before Laurelle came home, but he just said, 'Leave that to me. I've got commercial cleaners and decorators standing by. You get the cat out.'

I'm happy to say that after a bit of excitement and an hour of near catastrophe, I managed to inject some sedative into the poor tom cat and remove it from the premises. I think I took the tom cat back to the clinic, castrated it and let it go near Kevin's place a few days later. It would find its way home and would hopefully stay there.

As I packed up my equipment and walked down the drive to my car, a commercial cleaners' van was already arriving with a large team of cleaners. I didn't envy any of them their job, but Kevin was a man with a mission.

Laurelle came home in a plaster and was none the wiser, as far as Kevin has ever admitted.

IMA DREAMER — PA

Being involved professionally with thoroughbreds and trotters and with the retail manager at the Graham Veterinary Club, Kevin O'Brien, a thoroughbred trainer, meant the inevitable happened. Chick and I, along with four other couples, leased a young colt named Ima Dreamer for Kevin to train. Kevin naturally had some interest in this arrangement and also in the choice of horse we would lease.

Those who know about racehorses appreciate that many of them have ridiculous names or what sound like very inappropriate names. However, I am told that many of these names arise when the horse is still a foal and something about its nature stimulates a particular name. One can understand how Bone Crusher or Fiscal Madness might have acquired their names, so we really should have thought twice about the horse when we found out what he was called. He was without doubt the world's most appropriately named horse. Ima Dreamer was a friendly grey thoroughbred and I cannot recollect what his breeding was or where he came from but we ended up with him.

After he arrived Kevin put him into training and at the appropriate time, and when Kevin felt he was due for his first start, the syndicate travelled over to Nelson with great excitement to watch his first race. Some of us went the night before and had some pre-race entertainment. We were all quite excited and reasonably optimistic that he might do well. Who knows, we could have another Phar Lap on our hands. 'He's worth a bet,' said Kevin.

He certainly was, as the tote was paying around $50 for a win and $30 for a place. Obviously no one knew the potential of Ima Dreamer — or perhaps they did. We all bet heavily, something like $5 each way, and went back to the stand excited horse owners, calculating our likely winnings. Older and experienced members of the racing fraternity were giving us knowing looks. Obviously our heavy late betting had had a significant effect because the payout on the tote for Ima Dreamer had crashed. Perhaps our obvious enthusiasm and insider knowledge of the horse influenced those nearby and others put a bet on him as well. We recalculated our winnings, but they still looked not too bad.

Suddenly the horses were off. There is a grey on the outside of the leading bunch and he is running smoothly. We cheer Ima Dreamer on and by the first corner he has moved up to third place. However, we are becoming a little concerned by now as no one has yet heard his name from the race caller. I happened to look back to the starting box and suddenly a grey leaps out. Sure enough, it's that bloody dreamy horse. It's a short race and as the leading horses, including the other grey, flash past the winning post, Dreamer comes around the corner into the final straight, legs going in all directions. While our first start was a little embarrassing, it gave others plenty of amusement.

Kevin worked on Dreamer's starting technique and when he

had determined all was well we set off to Rangiora for the next start. We were full of excitement and convinced that this time he would be successful, or at the very least, run well. After all he had not shown he was slow — just slow getting away. 'Definitely worth a bet,' said Kevin.

So again we bet heavily on Ima Dreamer, who was paying at least $3 for a place, and then went and waited in the stand with some excitement but perhaps a little less loud enthusiasm than at the first race. The announcer came on and was doing the preliminaries for the race when suddenly a horse bursts through its starting gate. There is no way this horse is going to be late getting away. It's a brilliant start, the gate doesn't hold him back and he's away, but no other horses are. Naturally it's Ima Dreamer. The jockey finally pulls him up just within the required distance and he is led back to and put back in the starting box. Soon after he has returned the race actually starts. This time he got away when he was meant to. Not late, not early, right on time. Unfortunately he had already run a race and though he won that one, it did not really count. In the real race he came in last, again, and by at least 10 lengths.

So we all snuck home a little disappointed with our promising racehorse. However, we consoled ourselves by assuring each other he had not really been tested yet. At his first run he had given the rest of the field a head start. Well more like 30 body lengths, and that didn't count. The second he had already run a race while the rest had only just warmed up. So that didn't count. The third race in a couple of weeks' time was to be in Blenheim, his home ground. This time he would be ready. Just to make sure I filled him with every legal vitamin and tonic I could find and Kevin pulled out all his secret training techniques. By the end of the second week Ima Dreamer was looking a picture. The day arrived and Kevin reckoned he was ready and 'worth a bet all right'. This time we wouldn't be disappointed.

Ima Dreamer got a dream start. He had a good draw with the inside running and was in the leading bunch for the first few paces. We could see him easily on the far side of the track right against the fence but very soon we could also see all the others going around outside him. Steadily he made his way to the back of the field and by the start of the corner was sitting in his favourite position. He obviously felt comfortable there. Ima Dreamer thundered past the finishing post several lengths last, having failed to make up any ground on the field, including the second to last horse, which had pulled up lame.

Our horse's racing future was not looking promising. He had failed to show any turn of speed at all. He certainly didn't appear to be a sprinter and there was no indication that he was a stayer either. Kevin O'Brien thought he knew what the problem was. 'I'm sure his balls are his problem. He's got huge ones and they have to be getting in the way and are interfering with his stride. You see how his legs go in all directions. We need to "nick" him.'

I had never heard of testes getting in the way, but we were prepared to try anything. Someone also suggested that perhaps being a stallion he liked to run behind the other horses rather than in front. Whatever, getting rid of them couldn't make him slower and shedding a couple of stone might help. His prospect of taking on stallion duties in the future did not look too bright and as the owner was happy that we went ahead, I arranged to do the job the following week.

In the meantime two of the wives of syndicate members were fascinated to learn that our horse was going to have his gonads removed. They had never seen such an operation and wanted to know how it was done. Could they watch?

'Of course,' I said. 'Be at the back of the racecourse at 9.30am next Tuesday.' They arrived in good time and watched with fascination when I gave Ima Dreamer a tranquiliser injection into the jugular vein in his neck and then followed with the thiopentone anaesthetic. A few seconds afterwards he slumped to the ground, lying there motionless.

'Is he dead?' one of them shrieked.

Nowadays we tend to use combinations of new generation anaesthetics that allow for a very smooth induction and recovery. Animals go under without any struggle and stand up with minimum staggering after the anaesthetic has worn off. For many years veterinarians used one of the best available and that was thiopentone. Because it was a short-acting anaesthetic, we had to work fairly quickly when doing jobs like castrations. It did have a drawback in that recovery was slow and could be a bit wild with the horse trying to stand up while still very groggy. Once up it might then stagger around for 10 to 20 minutes, which some found a little distressing to watch. One of the other effects of thiopentone was that horses, once they crumpled to the ground as the anaesthetic kicked in, might not breathe for a minute or two. Nothing to really worry about but my two onlookers were concerned.

'Probably,' I replied. 'I need to work very quickly and I might be able to save him.' Making a bit of a show of running around, tying his off-hind leg up to his neck, and then quickly cutting his scrotum with a scalpel and using an emasculator, we had both testes out within a minute or two. About the time the tension came on the testes and the emasculator crushed the spermatic cord, Ima Dreamer took a large breath.

'He's alive,' they shouted from behind me. 'Well done, Pete. You've saved him.'

Both women were somewhat perplexed by the whole procedure. They didn't appreciate that while he was lying there dying I had castrated him and they really thought the whole procedure was a little barbaric. They couldn't explain how they thought it should be done. They just couldn't believe it could be done that way.

Well, Ima Dreamer soon stood up and started grazing, perhaps a little staggery, but not nearly as concerned about the event as the two women were. A few weeks later he went back into training and a couple of months later he had his fourth and last start. He came last again.

Ima Dreamer really was a hopeless racehorse but he did turn out to be quite a good polo pony. He couldn't run but he could stop and turn. We just didn't appreciate his talent.

The day after I had castrated Ima Dreamer, I posted his testes to Chris Borrie, one of the women watching the operation and the one most concerned about the event. I didn't hear anything until the next weekend when Chick and I were having a dinner party for a few friends. Chris and Ron Borrie, a local dentist, just happened to have been invited and brought along a tray of lamingtons. They were beautifully sculptured lamingtons, small ones and neatly coated in coconut icing, and I couldn't wait to try them. They were handed around with coffee after the meal and I couldn't understand why I got the first pick and why the whole room went suddenly quiet as I was about to take a dainty bite out of the corner of my lamington. On closer inspection it didn't seem to have quite the right texture and it was awfully heavy for its size. A little bit of serum weeping through the coconut gave the show away. Ron had gone to considerable length to cut each testis up into nice neat cubes and I almost fell for it.

Surprisingly the same syndicate was persuaded by Kevin to take on another horse after Ima Dreamer took on polo duties. This time a slightly more classy horse, a filly called Weymana, entered Kevin's stables. With a flash name like that she should have done well. She had three starts and finished with a fourth. She did show some promise but we were concerned about her heart and an ECG confirmed she had a fairly serious heart condition.

Obviously we just were not meant to be racehorse owners: Weymana was found dead in the paddock shortly after being put out to pasture for a spell.

For all of us that was the end of our involvement with owning or leasing racehorses. Some years later, however, my brother Tim asked me if I would like to join a syndicate of six others in a very well-bred thoroughbred. I told him in no uncertain terms that I was not at all interested. 'Been there — done that. I know all about getting involved with thoroughbreds.'

'You're a fool, Pete. This horse is very well bred. It's one of Jo Wilding's best bred horses and we just need one more partner.'

'No, Tim, you're the fool. It will cost heaps of money and I definitely don't want anything to do with it. Don't ask me again.'

Sure enough, Fiscal Madness had a long and successful racing career.

GYMNASTICS AND TESTICLES — PJ

I was never much of a gymnast. Early schoolboy experiences of shivering in cold Dunedin school gyms, with dozens of skinny teenage boys being made to vault the wooden horse; it all put me off the whole gymnastic thing.

Give me a rugby ball, a cricket ball, plenty of running around and competition — that always turned my wheels, but I could never perform a cartwheel or even a decent handstand, let alone an aerial somersault, forwards or backwards.

But I am proud to say that before I became too bodily inflexible, I once, and once only, did the best backward somersault you've ever seen. The fact that it was involuntary, had outside assistance and left me bruised and furious is of no moment. The fact is, I did it.

It was a fine Marlborough January day as I turned into Kit and Margie Sandall's property, Upton Fells in the Medway, a tributary of the Awatere River. It's a winding, dusty road, and it was always nice to reach my destination and get on with the job.

The job today was checking the rams. Every year, most commercial farmers and all stud ram breeders have their rams' testicles checked. We looked for variation in size and tone, and especially for lumps, which could mean brucellosis or actinobacillosus, two bacterial diseases which can lead to infertility, or at least sub-fertility. It's an important task. One ram can serve up to 200 ewes in a season, although in Marlborough's extensive hill and high country runs, ratios of one to 100 or even less are more common. An infertile ram can have a big effect on the lambing percentage, and if there are several, as can happen if brucellosis is in the flock, it can be disastrous.

The job of checking them entails approaching a race full of rams from behind, squatting behind each ram, and palpating each ball, one hand on left and right.

It's a simple but important task. Because rams are strong and sometimes aggressive, and merino rams have spectacular and very hard, curved horns, it's usual to have the farmer in the race as well, keeping the rams tight together so they can't move around. Many is the time I have waddled after a moving ram on my knees, both hands firmly clasped on his crown jewels, but this wasn't what we needed. We needed them standing still.

Kit Sandall had spent some years on a farm in Western Australia in his youth. He'd met his lovely wife Margie there, and he'd picked up a few Aussie tricks as well. The big sheep studs in Australia have narrow 'ram races' where those who do the checking and selecting of rams can walk along from outside the race, looking at the wool, the head and so on. These races are strictly one ram wide, very different from the wider races New Zealand farmers have in their sheep yards, where they can walk their way up a race three or four sheep wide, drenching or whatever the task of the day is.

So picture a narrow race, one ram wide, about 20 metres long, packed with 25 or 30 horned merino rams.

Picture also the vet, the writer, yours truly, crouched at the back of the pen, palpating the cojones of the first ram. After checking the first, I have to squeeze past that ram and push him back to give myself some space to work on the next one. Checking that the first one, now finished with, won't charge my vulnerable and unprotected back, is Marty.

Marty, Alan Martin to his mother, is in his forties at the time of my visit. He is a bachelor, a red-haired, friendly man. He has worked on farms all his life, and has been Kit's right-hand man at Upton Fells for many years. Marty has a small block of land at Okaramio, 60 or 70 kilometres away from Upton Fells, to the north of Blenheim, but he spends most of his nights during the week at Upton Fells. He is part of the property, part of the furniture if you like. He is a good man but no farm manager, and is not as acutely aware of his responsibilities as, say, Kit is. Or any owner-operator.

I'd known Marty for some years and we got on well. When I arrived that day, he was there alone as I slipped into my boots and overalls for the job.

'Where's Kit, Marty?' I enquire.

'He's taken Margie for a holiday down the Sounds,' says Marty. 'A rare occurrence.' And he grins broadly.

Like many high country farmers, Kit is a farmer first and second, and holidays aren't all that frequent. Marty is enjoying seeing his boss having a break.

As I begin the job on the rams, I am acutely aware of the vulnerable position I am in.

'It's your job to watch my back, Marty. Keep those buggers from charging when I'm not looking.'

'No problem, Pete,' he chuckles.

I've done about eight or 10 rams, no problems, nice tight

testes, no lumps. Each time, I squeeze past the one I've done, past the big curved horns, and Marty pushes them back down the race from outside. The race is about a metre high, so he can reach over easily.

As I move on to the next one, Marty is telling me a story about dog trialling, something he dabbles with in his spare time.

And then instinct, a sixth sense, makes me look up. Marty is gazing into the distance to the east. The rams behind me are to the west. I glance behind me. The last ram, the one I've just checked has his head up, five or six metres away. He wants to be with his mates, who are ahead of me. He is on the point of charging. It is a fearsome sight.

As he charges at me, I turn towards him, put both hands on the rails, and rapidly lever myself up with my arms, lifting my feet up and towards my horny adversary so he can pass underneath me, as he tries to reach the safety of his colleagues in front. For a split second I think I've made it but as he reaches me, he leaps in the manner that escaping sheep will, as they cross an open gateway. His terminal velocity must be 20 kilometres per hour, about five and a half metres per second. He weighs about 80 kilograms. Never good at Newtonian physics, I can still tell you that is a lot of applied force when it hits your unsupported feet.

The effect was terrific, turning me into an immediate backward somersault and cracking my unprotected head on the steel angle iron lining the right-hand rail, as I collapsed into the race. The ram thundered over my torso and face as I lay supine and stupefied in the bottom of the race.

There was a mighty roar from Marty.

'Jeez, I wish I'd had a video camera!' he shrieked, delighted with the effect. It's always nice to see the vet humiliated.

I was furious.

'You stupid ginger-headed bastard,' I shouted. 'Your job is to protect me, not to take photos of me.'

I pulled myself to my feet, dusted myself off and finished the job in fuming silence.

Marty knew he'd cocked up, and nothing much was said for the next half hour, or even as I packed up and left.

Afterwards, I could see the humour, and Marty and I remained on good terms until his sudden, untimely death some years later.

In fact, neither of us mentioned it ever again. I'm glad there was no one else there. The story might have grown into something really spectacular.

DEER CAPTURE DAYS — PA

After deer farming was legalised in 1969 a live animal captured from the wild became a far more valuable commodity than a dead one and the easiest way to capture a live animal was by helicopter. Various methods were used, the most basic being bull-dogging where men launched themselves from a helicopter onto a running deer and wrestled it to the ground. Legs were tied and the deer then bagged. The two most common methods, however, were darting and netting. With darting, tranquillisers were delivered via a syringe fired from a dart gun and with netting, nets were fired from net guns usually hand-held by the shooter in the helicopter.

Another common method was by setting up deer traps in clearings in the bush where deer frequently grazed, or on the edge of bush where deer could be enticed into the trap by planting a favourite of theirs in the trap such as a brassica, or baiting the trap with food such as branches of the broadleaf tree, a much sought-after plant. Once in the trap the deer would usually trigger a trip wire that set a spring-loaded gate to shut behind them. These traps would work very well on some properties and many farmers got into deer farming through capturing deer in this manner. It was while my brother Tim and I were setting up such a trap on his property that I managed to put a set of wire cutters through my mouth and knock out three of my front teeth. Our scheme was to capture and sell any deer caught — they were worth up to $3000 each and we were going to get rich. However, that was not to be. It was an expensive trap, having cost a fair bit on materials and a huge dental bill, and we never caught a single animal.

I became involved with deer capture at the time deer farming was just getting under way. I got into this somewhat by accident. My brother-in-law, Bill Reid, was a helicopter pilot and at the time tranquilliser darts fired from helicopters seemed to be the method of choice for capturing live deer. However, to get hold of the highly potent drugs required either a veterinary degree or a special licence. I supplied the drug and became the third member — another set of eyes to find the deer, bagger of tranquillised deer, and experimenter of drugs — of a reasonably successful live deer capture team.

Whatever means of capture we used, bull-dogging, darting or netting, the deer still had to be bagged. They were first of all tied up using padded leather leg straps and then placed in specially designed bags that allowed them to be comfortably slung beneath the helicopter. Bull-dogged or netted deer were given a tranquilliser to put them in a state of 'peace and tranquillity' while the darted deer were given an antidote which allowed partial recovery from the heavy sedation they were under. Once a load of three or four deer had been caught, we would head back to base and release them into a shed where they were watered and fed and closely observed for several days before being transported by road to a farm. It never failed to amaze me how quickly red deer adapted to domestication.

One of the problems with using tranquilliser darts was the drug itself. It just took too long to work, especially in a highly excited deer that could have been chased over some distance. Hovering in a helicopter for several minutes watching the one darted deer from a distance and waiting for it to go down was costly and meant that other opportunities were lost. With good Kiwi ingenuity, combinations of drugs that worked quicker and tracking devices attached to the darts that allowed the 'shooter' to come back after an appropriate time and more easily find the deer were soon developed. However, other methods were also being used including netting. We eventually used a combination of all methods depending on circumstances.

We first experimented with a huge net attached beneath the Hughes 500 helicopter and fired by the pilot. Although I think Bill got a big thrill out of using it, it was a little cumbersome. Missing meant several minutes retrieving the net, finding somewhere where we could land, and then reloading. More successful were the smaller nets fired by blanks from a modified shot-gun or .303. Several nets could be stored in the helicopter and my job, sitting in the back of the Hughes 500, was to look out for deer and hand the nets to the shooter as he used them. If there was more than one deer netted, or more to net, I would leap out and strap the legs and bag the first deer and then give it its tranquilliser. We felt the tranquilliser was necessary because it could be some hours before we were able to release them at the holding facility. Problems developed with over-stressed deer, and some tranquillisers reduced the incidence of these, including a 'tying-up' syndrome, the end result of overheating. With this condition severe muscle cramping and kidney damage would invariably result in death of the animal.

There were plenty of exciting moments. All of the deer capture took place in the northwest corner of the South Island — wild, magnificent, uninhabited country. Much of that country is only rarely visited by the occasional intrepid tramper and fishermen or geologists. One incident occurred when one of the four net weights jammed in its barrel under the helicopter. The rest of the net hooked itself on a ledge of a near precipice while the stag galloped off into the bush. We were therefore attached to the land and couldn't move. The rotor blades were dangerously close to the cliff and Bill could not rest a skid on the ledge. The shooter, Wal, eased his way along the skid to try and release the weight but couldn't. He then decided the best option was to leap off onto the ledge. That resolved the problem to a certain extent. The change in weight distribution meant the 500 pulled up and back — the barrel broke off, the helicopter flipped momentarily upside down, and Wal knocked himself out on the rock. After Bill had composed himself and I had sorted myself out in the back, we returned to carefully pick up the net and a dazed Wal, bleeding from the head. That was enough deer capture for the day.

On another occasion at the end of a relatively unsuccessful day, we came across a sow and her litter. Wal and I leapt out and raced off in different directions and eventually caught one each. As I leapt back onto the skid and grabbed hold of a short length of rope next to the shooter's seat with my left hand, Bill moved off. Holding onto the piglet with my right hand I placed him onto the floor in front of the seat. When the helicopter was a good 100 feet up and Bill was looking for Wal, the piglet decided to latch onto my thumb. The power of self-preservation overcame the pain and I did manage to hang onto that rope but the pain was excruciating and worse still when I tore him off and hurled him into the back of the helicopter.

While most of the deer were eventually caught by net, I did have to resort to bull-dogging a couple of times. One day Wal was having a bad day. We had half a dozen nets that could be rapidly loaded into the net gun. This allowed repeat shots if a miss occurred or if more than one animal required netting. We were chasing a particularly wily hind this day and she had been able to avoid all the nets shot at her. These were now littering a considerable area of a mountainside. With no nets left Wal had to resort to bull-dogging but he also ended up as a blob on the landscape and the hind raced on. It was now my turn but luckily she was getting rather exhausted by this time and didn't put up too much of a fight after I landed on her. While she was not the only one I bull-dogged, we avoided using that method of capture if we could. It was definitely the most physical way of deer capture and I doubt very much that my body would be up to handling that sort of treatment these days.

Those deer capture days were exciting ones and a good introduction to the effects of different drugs on deer and their amazing adaptability to domestication. However, it appears my deer capture days were not over. Recently, and 30 years later, I got involved with capturing wild deer again, this time for a very different reason. I had been involved with some work with Ivor Yockney from Landcare Research, who was doing some novel, ground-breaking research into working out home territories of wild pigs and deer and their use as sentinel animals for TB. The work was on Muzzle Station in the Clarence Valley for the pigs, and Molesworth Station for the deer.

With pigs we released animals in which Mary Bowron and I had implanted transmitters and in some, a GPS unit. Mary, a more recent veterinary graduate and a local, bucked the trend of most of her generation and is keen on the large animal work. These days she does most of the practical hands-on farm work in our practice while I work very hard at avoiding it. She is also very game and will take on everything thrown at her and even delights in flying with me. Getting her to help with the surgery in the field in possibly one of the more isolated areas, with Tapuae-o-Uenuku as a beautiful backdrop, is not a problem.

The pigs had been sourced from a wild TB-free population in the Marlborough Sounds and bred in captivity. Once they were old enough we operated on them, inserting implants under the skin, and a few days later released them at specific sites. They were later shot and post-mortemed to determine whether they had picked up TB after they had been released, and what territory they had covered from the information recorded on the GPS. If they had TB lesions, then it could be assumed they had picked it up from eating TB vectors such as possums that had died in the area they had travelled over. Poisoning possums, the most important wild vector of TB, could be then restricted to specific areas rather than the expensive blanket poisoning jobs which have become somewhat unpopular.

We darted wild deer from a helicopter as in the early days. We took a blood sample, tagged them and attached a collar with a GPS unit and a transmitter so that they could eventually be tracked down. After this they were given the antidote, which meant that within a couple of minutes they had recovered, stood up and then usually just trotted off, apparently not too fazed by the whole experience. This is the first such work that has been done on deer in the wild in New Zealand. Eventually they will need to be captured again to retrieve the units.

However, the job was just as I remember it — the smell of Jet A1, the excitement of looking for the deer, then the chase, and the eventual capture. All was the same except this helicopter seemed harder to climb in and out of, the deer seemed bigger and stronger, and the mountains were steeper.

OF ROOFS AND FINGERS — PJ

It had been a bad day, cold and wet. I was on a duty weekend, and Saturday had been full of emergencies. After a full morning doing routine consultations and some minor surgery — cats with abscesses, dogs with corneal ulcers, that sort of thing — I had then gone to see a lame horse before going back to the surgery for another dog or two. Early evening I had been called to do a caesarean section in a cow well up the Wairau Valley. An hour's drive, at least two hours doing the surgery, a flat battery because I'd left the car door open and the lights on, and an hour home. I was bushed. I got home late, ate dinner and headed for bed.

When the phone went at 1am I was dead to the world, so much so that I must rely on Ally's account of the early parts of this story. The client was a lovely person, one of my favourite clients, a sympathetic and understanding woman from Picton. At least I knew I would have sensible assistance, and that her husband would almost certainly be there to help as well. Ally recognised the name, but as she always did, answered the call professionally and with some degree of protection for me. She knew I was pretty knackered.

She maintains that when she handed me the phone, I mumbled 'Hello' and went through the diagnostic motions, and then fell asleep with the phone clutched to my chest. She rescued me and clamped the phone to my ear again, so that I was able to hear the problem. A whelping bitch, one pup out, but with nothing happening for the last hour.

Now a whelping bitch is always an interesting problem. Two hours between pups is considered the absolute maximum before the bitch needs veterinary intervention. That can take the form of manual assistance, maybe with the use of the hormone oxytocin to stimulate contractions, or a caesarean section, meaning a general anaesthetic and full abdominal surgery to deliver the pups. With many of our dog-breeding clients, we would encourage them to take blood samples prior to mating, so that the date of ovulation was known. With that knowledge, it's a simple matter to know the date the pups are expected, but it is hard to convince dog breeders to do this. Many still haven't grasped the notion that veterinary science has moved on, and that the actual mating date can be removed from ovulation day by as much as seven days. Ovulation day is the key. Once that's known, everything else follows, with small variations. So, if we knew the expected date, and if on that date they weren't starting labour, I would encourage the owner to bring the bitch in during daylight hours so we could make a full assessment. That way we could do the caesarean, if necessary, in the day, with a full complement of nursing staff on hand.

At night, by oneself and with an anxious owner on hand, it can be a very challenging procedure. The bitch needs an intravenous anaesthetic, then must be intubated to go on the gas anaesthetic machine, and all surgery has to be done in a sterile fashion. So it's not something to look forward to in the middle of the night, and many times my wife or children assisted me with these fascinating but demanding pieces of surgery.

But back to my weekend on duty.

We agreed that the owner would keep an eye on the situation and ring me if there was still no action in an hour. If that happened I would have to perform a C-section.

Sleep claimed me until 3am when the phone went again, and again I must rely on Ally's account. She says it went like this: 'Hello. Yes, hmmmm,' mumbled advice, and then sounds of snoring as I fell asleep again. The next thing I remember was a thump: Ally had hit the floor and was rolling about laughing. That finally woke me up.

With whelping bitches, there's a thing called Ferguson's reflex and it is a handy trick that allows owners and vets to help their bitch produce the pups when things have ground to a halt. Eliciting Ferguson's reflex involves stroking the roof of the bitch's vagina with your finger and this often stimulates contractions in a labour that has stalled. I have used it many times with success, and it can save a trip to the vet for the owner. But this night, I wasn't quite on form, as the perceptive reader might have guessed. Ally maintains that I said, 'Yes indeed, Mrs McTavish. Now, have you tried stroking the roof with the finger of your vagina?'

During the caesarean that followed, and the ensuing weeks as the pups came in for check-ups and vaccinations, I fully expected Mrs Mac to tackle me over the events of that night. Sweet woman, she never embarrassed me by so much as mentioning it. And Ally still shrieks with uncontrolled mirth whenever she recalls it, which is embarrassingly often.

FAINTERS — PA

It is not all that surprising that many people feel uncomfortable in the presence of blood and guts and the smells of antiseptics, anaesthetics and myriad other concoctions — all necessary in a well-functioning surgery. However, what does sometimes surprise me is who is most susceptible. More often than not it is a man. Quite often it has been one who has spent the day pig hunting, sticking pigs, getting his dog ripped up, doing some hasty surgery in the field to push back a piece of fern-covered dog gut and using his jersey as a bandage, carrying the dog for miles to the ute and rushing it to the clinic at some ungodly hour to be 'fixed up'. Preliminaries have to be dispensed with — it is late, the dog has lost a heap of blood, he needs a drip (intravenous fluids and blood if possible) and he needs his wounds cleaned and repaired. Out comes the bottle of thiopentone, suck the required amount into a syringe, place a decent-sized needle on syringe, syringe towards the ceiling and expel unwanted air bubbles. It is about this time that you become aware the owner has stopped talking, is looking very pale, sweating heavily and complaining about how hot it is in the cold little surgery. You are about to lose your assistant.

So single-handedly you anaesthetise, intubate and hook up the dog to the anaesthetic machine, put him on a saline drip, and then clean up what, underneath a fairly small superficial skin wound, is a severely damaged and contaminated abdominal wall and intestines. Good surgical repair requires much cleaning of contaminated tissue and cutting away damaged or dead tissue. The actual surgical repair is often a relatively small percentage of the time spent on the dog. And no matter the value of the dog, and whatever the owner's history for paying for services, you are a professional and you do the best job you can.

George Kyle was a giant of a man. Late one Sunday evening I received a call from him. 'Is that the vet?' The usual start to many telephone calls with no apology for disturbing my evening. 'Yeah, I've just got home. Me best dog is pretty cut up. His guts is hanging out. Can I bring him in?'

Of course I couldn't refuse and telling him to give the dog a disprin wasn't going to work. I met George at the clinic and proceeded to examine his dog on the surgery table. Indeed his guts were hanging out, but luckily he had not lost too much blood. It was going to be quite a long job, firstly to clean up the contaminated intestines, then to repair the wound caused by the tusks of a boar. Luckily the intestines, although covered in bits of foliage and dirt, were not ruptured. But while superficially the wound didn't look too bad, there was bound to be some major internal damage. George was covered in blood and was starting to regale me with stories of the day. It was all tough man talk, but George was putty in my syringe-filled hand. He went very quiet and then staggered out the door and collapsed against some cupboards and drawers the moment the syringe went vertical. There was a horribly expensive tearing, crashing sound as he bounced off the cupboards and fell sprawling over an examination table. He recovered after a few minutes and quietly sneaked out for a fag and then off home. Later the cupboards needed replacing and the table required some major repairs.

On another occasion I was removing an intestinal obstruction. Two of the more common causes of intestinal obstructions in working dogs are ear tags and corn cobs. The bigger Allflex or Nu-Zee type tags must have an irresistible earwaxy, scabby flavour to them when they fall out and dogs can't resist them. They can roll up and get stuck halfway down the intestinal track and can be a real challenge for diagnosis, often undetected even with good abdominal palpation and radiographs. The classic symptoms of vomiting and not passing any faeces are not observed because ingesta or gut contents can still pass through. On the other hand solid obstructions such as stones, bones, golf balls or corn cobs are frequently easily palpated and picked up on radiographs.

On this occasion it was a particularly busy day, PJ was out doing some farm calls, Jill, our receptionist and assistant nurse, was busy trying to do both jobs and I was interrupted while in the middle of the operation by Keith, a drug company representative. The operation was to remove a three to four centimetre length of corn cob that had been stuck for too long, causing necrosis (death) of about 10 centimetres of intestine. All dead tissue had to be cut away and two ends of nice healthy intestine then needed rejoining. Keith liked to talk — lots. But I thought I could make use of him and allow Jill to get on with some other work requiring urgent attention. She was a total multi-tasker and could handle most things. Holding a set of bowel clamps so that the two ends of intestine were nicely apposed would allow for easier suturing and was not an onerous task for any assistant — or so I thought. 'Keith — go and wash your hands well, use that brown stuff in the bottle beside the taps and dry your hands with the paper towels on the wall there and come and make yourself useful.'

Keith obliged and did what I asked of him and held the bowel clamps just where I needed them, rotating slightly as I worked my way around the intestine and he still talked — for a while. I then found I had to keep asking him not to keep moving his hands his way all the time because it meant I had to lean further over the table to keep suturing. I soon became aware that all was not well with Keith — Keith had gone very pale, Keith was sweating heavily, and Keith was not talking. I was about to lose another assistant. Sure enough he was now on a rapid slide down the wall, whites of eyes only showing in a deathly pale face, tongue out, not a pretty sight, but he diligently stuck to his duty and hung on to those bowel clamps. Intestines tumbled out of the dog's abdomen and over the edge of the table and lay along with the bowel clamps, swabs, drapes, and bits of resected gut on Keith's comatose body. I retrieved the intestines and instruments after checking that Keith was breathing — well, making little moaning noises at least. Jill returned to help finish the job but not before unceremoniously dragging Keith out of the way. Keith finally came to and looked with glazed eyes at the mess of swabs and resected dog intestine, corn cob and ooze soiling the front of his nice clean company jersey: 'What the hell happened?'

I have always envied PJ's skill at detecting when to react to a fainting owner, stepping in to catch them right at the moment their legs start to buckle and gently lowering them to the floor. I'm not too sure about male fainters but as far as I am aware he has never failed a fainting female yet. As for me I usually only became aware something was amiss when they disappeared from my peripheral vision and I heard the thud-thuck as body followed by head hit the floor.

(PJ: This last paragraph is pure wishful thinking on PA's part, and has no foundation in fact.)

TRAFFIC COPS — PJ

I'm not very proud of this story, but all things can have a funny side if you want to see it, so I think it's worth telling.

In 1998, I had a disagreement with a policeman. It wasn't actually a two-way altercation, more a unilateral disagreement.

It was my birthday, and we'd had a dinner for everyone from our practice at the Blenheim Club, a crusty, semi-stately fornicatorium/mausoleum built as a gentlemen's club in 1903. The old walls are sheathed in stained rimu panels. The ceilings are impossibly high, and the place in those days was old, cold and ugly. It's had quite a facelift now and is old, warm and ugly, but there is still a musty Victorian reek to the place, and the entrenched conservatism of the place is enshrined in the portraits of the Queen, Winston Churchill, and Lord Freyberg which adorn the walls.

But in those days, it was a pretty cheap place to hire out, and the managers of recent times have provided excellent fare when asked to do meals, so we chose to go there for our function.

On the night in question the meal was excellent, and by

midnight there were four couples left, possibly the partners of our practice (by then The Vet Centre) and a senior staff member, but I really can't remember; we were cleaning up a few bottles of red at the time, and the memory blurs just a little. There was a discussion about calling into someone's place on the way home, and because Ally wished to go home, while I thought socialising was a good idea, I drove. Foolishly, as I'd had a few. The result was the unilateral disagreement with a policeman, which I mentioned, an appearance in court and loss of licence for six months.

Now, while it's not the end of the world, it's a degrading, humiliating and embarrassing experience. Which it should be, and lesson definitely learnt.

The real problem as a rural veterinarian is that you really do need your car. So another visit to court means that it is possible to get a licence, but there are severe restrictions as to how said car can be used. Only for work. Only a certain route to be taken from home to work. A log to be kept of all work calls, and the farmer to be rung when leaving to go there, so the gendarmerie can check on you. All very tiresome.

And the last restriction is — no passengers. I'm not sure why, but no passengers.

We fast forward three months. A young, very able and enthusiastic student is spending two weeks in the clinic. Geoff is so keen, he comes in the weekends to get more experience with the on-duty vet. It is Marlborough Wine Festival Day in February. It's always a hot day, and there are always a lot of police around. I think they spend all of January cloning them somewhere, so there'll be enough for the Marlborough Wine Festival. Every driver leaving the festival is stopped 100 metres down the road and breath tested.

I, however, am virtuously doing my weekend on duty, slightly darkly, thinking of everyone else having fun at Brancott Vineyard, scene of the festival.

Geoff the student has helped me on several cases. At 4pm comes a call from a farmer's daughter in the Wairau Valley, 40 minutes drive up the valley. She has a horse with colic, abdominal pain and discomfort. This can be a serious symptom for a horse. Geoff wishes to come. I'm not supposed to take any passengers, but Geoff has been very helpful and I know all the cops will be at the wine festival site stopping the drivers about this time.

'Come on, Geoff, we'll be right.'

I have nothing against the police. They have a difficult job and some are my friends. But one or two, or possibly hundreds in the traffic division, can be just a little officious. The thought of stopping a restricted driver and finding he has a passenger would be a juicy prospect to some of these gentlemen and women. Just some, mind you. I have no doubt that some are thoroughly nice people, and can even read the newspaper, spot the Southern Cross, and appreciate the Finn Brothers. But not all.

Off we go, past the growing satellite town of Renwick, up the road running due west along the great fault line towards the Nelson Lakes and the West Coast. The hills to the south are bone dry, a sort of dusty clay colour, while those across the river to the north are green, alternatively clothed in scrub, exotic pine forest, and further up the valley, beautiful native beech forest reaching towards the bushline, before the rocky tops at 1500 to 2000 metres.

We are travelling along the edge of two of the earth's great crustal plates, the Pacific and the Australo-Indian continental plates, the joint of which, the main fault line, runs right through the centre of New Zealand, forming the Wairau Valley on the way.

I am anxious about this horse. The owner is not our usual client, preferring another vet, and I'm only average as a horse vet.

So I chat away to Geoff about what we may find.

Bloody hell! Red and blue flashing lights shoot past me going the other way towards town. I'm doing 125kmh or so and as I check in my rear vision mirror and see him stopping and turning to chase me, I get that adolescent feeling, so familiar when I was at school and always in trouble. What the hell are they doing up here? I can't do anything but keep on while the boys in blue put on a major spurt to catch me.

As they approach from behind, all lights, bells and whistles going, I pull resignedly into the side of the road and push the automatic drive lever to neutral. The cops pull up behind me.

I leap out, an urgent overalled figure, clearly on a mission of mercy. I'm going to tell these cops that this is urgent and I hope desperately that they don't check my licence with its big 'RESTRICTED' stamp across page six saying 'no passengers'. I stride along the grassy verge back towards the parked police car. As I raise my eyes to make contact with the gentlemen (there are two of them) I can see a look of horror in their eyes. They're not interested in me, but in my car which is gathering momentum, in reverse, towards their now parked car. I have put the gear lever into reverse, not neutral. Disaster on all fronts is looming.

Showing admirable presence of mind, Geoff pulls on the handbrake. The Subaru's rear bumper stops 10 centimetres from the police car.

'I'm in a hell of a hurry, there's a horse dying.' I am brusque, a man with a mission. I am also bluffing like hell.

The driver gulps, his eyes still wide with the shock of the near miss.

'Well, don't drive so fast,' he stammers. 'You were doing over 125.'

And he waved me away.

You don't often have a win at the right time. I was feeling a bit tail-down with the loss of licence and loss of face, but I felt a lot more cheerful after that.

A good student, that Geoff.

HOSPITAL VISITS — PA

Working with animals of any species can have its dangers but for some reason I seem to have had a little more time in hospital getting patched up or repaired from animal or unintentional self-inflicted injuries than Pete J. Perhaps he moves a little faster than I do. As a result there have been some times when he has had to hold the fort alone while I have lazed away. On occasions we have had to employ a locum or friend to help out. Once when I was out of action for several months a good friend of ours, Richard Lee from Hawke's Bay, kindly filled in for several weeks. This fact continues to haunt me to this day. I still get reminded by some farmers about the vet who worked for us while I was out of action. 'Hey Pete — remember that vet who was here when you were out of action after your prang. Gee, he was a good vet.' The insinuation being that he was better than me — which is quite possibly very true.

Anyway, Pete would regularly pay me visits. His good humour usually cheered me up but I'm not always sure to my advantage. Laughter and broken ribs are uncomfortable bedmates. On one occasion I was incapacitated following a rather uncomfortable procedure — a haemorrhoidectomy. While this procedure is uncomfortable for the recipient, if it is anything like removing anal glands from a ferret, it is probably also an unpleasant job for the surgeon. Anyway, before Pete left he attached a large 'Elizabethan collar' around my neck, which I had some difficulty removing. Elizabethan collars are collars we place around a cat's or dog's neck to stop them licking bandages or wounds or chewing out stitches. So here I am lying in bed with this collar and the nurses start coming in.

For the rest of my stay in hospital my name seemed to be associated with a good deal of mirth. The image of me trying to chew out my rectal sutures obviously amused them.

I always looked forward to Pete's visits over the years because he invariably brought along something to keep me amused, other than himself. If it wasn't a good book, it was very often a small flask of a medicinal compound — usually a special single malt. While it may not have been to doctor's orders I'm sure it always sped up recovery.

Together we have also visited friends in hospital. We decided one evening that my sister, who was having a prolonged and difficult first labour, needed some assistance. We arrived at the maternity ward and barged into the theatre all geared up with calving gowns, gumboots, calving jack, chains, and a bucket of lubricant and informed the concerned-looking doctor and nurses that we were here to assist. We are not too sure whether our offer was appreciated but believe the tense atmosphere in the theatre did improve a little.

Another time we thought we would cheer up a good mate who had had to undergo painful surgery for prostate cancer. We arrived at his room all properly attired in surgical gear. With gowns, masks, gloves, and surgery caps we would have been a little difficult to recognise. We carried a set of emasculators. Emasculators are what we use for castrating large animals with big testes. Castration is a very effective means of controlling prostate cancers. 'Hello, Mr Sheild. We have come to fix you.' (To fix = to neuter.) Tony was not terribly amused, which I guess is understandable under the circumstances. The nurses were bemused. We thought it was very funny.

One morning early in my career I was given a rather nasty kick below and inside the right knee while pregnancy testing some beef cows in, as was usual for the times, a rather substandard set of cattle yards. My response was understandable and included kicking the cow back, which did neither of us any good. By the time I had finished that herd and was trying to get my leggings and overalls off to drive to the next herd up the valley, my leg had swollen somewhat and the knee was not bending too well. I was developing a sizable haematoma. Methylated spirits cooled things down and after a while we drove to the next job. There were four herds to pregnancy test that day and by the time I had finished it was getting dark, my leg was very swollen, it was rather painful, and driving was not easy. I thought it prudent to perhaps drop in at the accident clinic and see if they could do anything to help. Otherwise it was going to be an uncomfortable night. So smelling like the contents of the rear end of a cow and still covered in much of it, I hobbled into the hospital. There was a young doctor on duty who took one look at my leg and decided that it definitely needed draining. This he said he would do with a large bore needle. For a good half hour he and every nurse in attendance scoured the hospital for a large bore needle. Now and then he would come back with some pathetic little needle and try and suck something out but this was a haematoma — clotted blood does not go through little holes.

Finally I said that I had a large needle or two in the car — would he like me to go and fetch one? His look was easy to read: 'You filthy man, all covered in and smelling of cow shit, how can you have a sterile large bore needle that I can use, in your car, when we can't find one in the hospital.'

He actually didn't say anything. I tried to explain to him that I was a vet, that I deal with big animals that have big veins, that I give big doses of thick stuff through big bore needles as quickly as I can because I don't have time to do it slowly. I need such needles because my patients refuse to sit around patiently reading books for an hour or two while I gently administer their treatments.

A couple of hours later and as the night wore on, he got the message and let me hobble back to the car and retrieve one of the hundreds of shiny two inch 14G needles, all individually sealed in their sterile packaging, which I carried. This allowed him to suck enough contents of the haematoma out to relieve the pressure and allow me to get some sleep that night. However, it was not until after an older rural doctor took one look at it the following morning, whipped out a scalpel, made a decent gash in my leg, and released a bucket full of clotted blood that things came right.

Brain injuries are more serious. Not only do they affect you but they affect your relationship with friends, families, clients and patients. It can be as tough on them as on you. After I had landed on my head on the tennis court in Kekerengu, as detailed earlier, and Rod Heard and his son Andrew had bravely hacked me out of the wreck, fuel dripping, engine hissing, I remained unconscious for several hours. Although I was back working and flying in three months, I do not believe I was back to my old self for a good two years. My short-term memory and ability to verbally express myself were affected, and for some reason I seemed to go through angry periods. I also 'lost it' with animals.

Many of us, but not all, who work with animals all our lives — farmers, stockmen, shearers, stock agents, stock truck drivers, vets, and others — will develop a unique rapport with animals. It may sound trite but we seem to communicate with them on a different sensory level. Our 'sixth' sense allows us to safely move amongst mobs of stock or handle individuals and even our presence will calm them. It's how and where you stand in relation to them, how you touch them, and how you look at them but most of all it is in the mind. One of the first lessons I tell a vet student getting work experience, when his or her presence seems to excite a group of animals, is to 'relax and think nice thoughts'. Despite what many think I do not believe lots of talking or trying to make soothing human noises to animals that have never learnt human commands is of any help. A command to calm down usually has the opposite effect.

So, it's all a bit of a mind thing. And after my knock on the head I lost the touch. My presence seemed to excite rather than relax animals, especially horses and deer. I lost the ability to be part of the mob and to anticipate their movements. I was no longer communicating with them. As a result I went back to my early practice days of arriving home with my daily quota of kicks and bites. Bluey Hope, an observant trotting trainer with whom I had regular contact, kept reminding me that I was 'not right yet'. He noticed that I was not handling his horses the same and having more difficulty doing basic stuff like examining, stomach tubing, or administering injections. His horses would not relax in my presence. It was also Bluey who one day said, 'Well done, Pete, you are back.'

My most recent, and hopefully last, visit to the hospital was for a perforated bowel and resultant peritonitis. It seemed to take an awfully long time before they had confirmed that I had a peritonitis — actually five days of increasing discomfort. In the meantime PJ and Stuart Burrough, who were regular visitors and were becoming increasingly concerned with the decline in my condition, were trying to encourage the medical profession to do something other than just observe.

At one stage I said to the surgeon in charge: 'Look, I can't tell you your job but if I was a dog I would by now be opening me up and having a look, and if I was a horse I would shoot me because this would be an animal welfare issue.' He didn't seem to find that amusing.

Eventually they confirmed I had peritonitis and I underwent

emergency surgery. Due to complications my recovery was somewhat prolonged but was undoubtedly smoothed by a daily visit from PJ along with a little bottle of a good tonic.

DOGS WHO WILL ALWAYS LOVE ME — PJ

This is not a chapter for the delicate reader. Those who don't like sex should quickly pass on to the next section ...

It all began with Hamish, a fine West Highland White dog. His owners, Jim and Peg McCallum, were good solid citizens, nothing fancy, retired and into breeding pups for sale. It was both a hobby and a bit of income for them. Jim was a good old chap, cheerful and one of the lads. Peg was the driving force, often a bit anxious, but always appreciative of what we did for her as vets.

What we did for her may shock some readers, but it is something a lot of vets do for their clients. We used to collect Hamish's semen, then artificially inseminate their on-heat bitch. I can't remember why they weren't allowed to do it naturally, but Peg and Jim had convinced themselves there was risk for the dog and preferred us to do it. (*PA: If I remember Hamish just didn't seem to know where to put his penis in the bitch. Remember we had to be quick as he was developing a bloody good erection before he had got onto the table.*)

Dear Hamish. We must have collected his semen at least 30 times, possibly a lot more, as the McCallums had a few breeding bitches. And after Hamish came another male dog, then another.

To digress a little, I must now include a short description of the process. To collect semen from a male dog, it helps if there is an oestrous (in heat) female present, dog that is. As the male gets interested, the vet has to extrude his — the dog's, that is — willing member from the sheath, popping out the swollen pars bulbis (the bit that gets them knotted), then cover the whole thing with a plastic collection cone, with a 10 ml collection tube wedged into the end of the cone. The vet then gently squeezes the pars bulbis a few times until the dog ejaculates into the cone, which channels the semen into the tube. It's actually a bit more complex than this, and there wasn't much training in the technique when I was student, but that's it in a nutshell.

Over the years this could lead to embarrassment and hilarity, depending on one's point of view. At one stage a very pretty young female vet was working for us. A farmer came in with his dog for an AI (artificial insemination), and the young woman ushered him into the consulting room and shut the door.

When they emerged 20 minutes later they were both looking embarrassed, and the client rapidly left the premises. On questioning our vet I found that the client had had to show her what to do. She did come from a good family.

Now you may think this is all a bit dodgy. My good friend Ron Crosby, a solicitor, once rang me when a mutual farmer client had just left his office, having just been to see me with his dog and bitch, before visiting Ron on legal business.

'You dirty bugger' was Ron's opening sentence. 'Is that what vets do? Disgusting!' All I could think of at the time was to splutter, 'Well, it's not half as dirty as the things you do in your profession,' which looking back may have been pretty accurate.

Ron's and my client was a prominent dog triallist. These people and their dogs are highly skilled and a top trial dog is a valuable breeding proposition, so many of them would come to see me when their breeding programme wasn't working.

The other large group we tendered our services for were the owners of show dogs, in itself a semi-major industry. Every weekend, this dedicated band groom their dog or dogs, put them in a trailer or the back of the car, or even a specially converted campervan, put on their glad rags (anything from suit and tie to best dancing regalia) and head off to a local or national show. Crufts, the British dog show, is the most famous of these, but it begins in the suburbs and goes local, provincial, national and international. It's their whole life and extremely important for them to have their dogs judged better than everyone else's.

While never fully attuned with the standards, desires and ethics of this last group, I was very much in tune with the sheep dog triallists. More importantly, the technical side of dog breeding appealed to me greatly, so in 1988 I began to educate myself to a higher level on the subject.

A week-long international course in Sydney sharpened my interest and led to a trip back to Melbourne, and eventually to a major round-the-world trip, meeting and working with a lot of the world experts in the field. Eventually I made several round-world trips, honing my skills, and absorbing knowledge in a field that was still pretty new. We were at the cutting edge.

An international trade in frozen dog semen was just beginning as I learnt how to cryopreserve, store, ship and importantly, to inseminate with it.

Unlike many mammalian species, dog semen does not freeze easily and the chemical/technical aspects of the process are still being unravelled and improved upon. I was lucky enough to strike a man in Pennsylvania and a professor in Sweden who were very advanced in their knowledge of that process, and critically, in the use of frozen semen.

As many of you will know, the bitch ovulates or cycles intermittently, every six to eight months at best. Freezing semen and inseminating with it is a tricky and expensive business, so a positive outcome is important to the breeder. Sadly, this is not always the case, often for technical reasons (as in human reproduction, we don't know all the answers yet), and in part because there is a very small pool of vets who are sufficiently educated in the subject. Even today, in the whole of New Zealand, there are possibly six vets who are so trained.

At the time I became interested, there were only one or two, so it was good personally and professionally to be at the forefront of one's field.

The common factor with nearly all of the dogs I collected semen from is that they all loved me. Afterwards that is, and usually for ever after.

The dogs who had been collected before would strain at the leash to get into the clinic when their owners brought them back next time. This was a fun place and I want to be there again, you could see them saying.

Returning to the good Hamish, he would rush into the clinic ahead of the McCallums, tongue out, almost smiling, and would go home afterwards, slightly wobbly, but very cheerful.

The problem in those early days, and I'm talking about the period from 1979 to 1982 at the Graham Vet Club, was that we didn't have very advanced equipment for the job.

The collection vessel was a five-ounce beer glass with the HANZ (Hotel Association of New Zealand) logo, a green circle with a map of New Zealand within, stamped on the side. It had no doubt been half-inched from the pub next door, but whatever its origin, it would be roughly warmed up in warm water, dried, then used as a receptacle for the fresh semen, until it was quickly drawn into a warm syringe and deposited into the waiting 'hot' bitch.

This glass had been around for many years, lived in the staffroom until required, and was avoided like the plague by all who worked there.

Unfortunately, and I'm sure it was accidental, the glass did get used for drinking from, once. We had a German student, a delightful young woman, working at the clinic for experience. She was with us for a week, possibly two, and I do remember her getting slightly crushed between two cows as I taught her pregnancy testing. She was brave and strong, however, and finished the job.

On the Friday afternoon she was to leave us, we decided to have a bit of a party after work. We got in a few beers and some of the clinic staff assembled with the young German. It wasn't difficult to round them up; she was rather gorgeous. At 5.30pm the door burst open. It was her male friend back from a week on the West Coast. For the sake of the story, she shall be Heidi and her friend, Gunter.

Gunter strode in almost clicking his heels, head up, very confident, the pride of Aryan youth.

'So,' he shouted, 'you are the wets!'

I'm sorry to say we all fell about laughing and I'm even sorrier to say that Gunter ended up drinking his beer from a five-ounce beer glass with a HANZ logo on the side. I'm sure that it had been washed.

There were plenty of other interesting moments around my new career as a canine reproductive vet, or what some of my less savoury friends called a 'dog walloper'.

I began to travel all over New Zealand collecting semen from dogs at clinics from Invercargill to Auckland. I would do the collecting, at most six or seven dogs a day, process the semen, chill and freeze it. All this took several hours and I was usually quite spent, in a manner of speaking, by the time the days were finished.

From time to time I would strike a dog who just couldn't deliver. It was noticeable that many of these dogs had over-anxious or overly dominant owners. I would often have to ask the owner to go out of the room or to stop talking while I collected. The dogs needed to concentrate on the job in hand, as it were.

Other dogs didn't like being in the vet clinic, a traumatic experience for them much as a visit to the dentist is for us. I could never imagine getting too randy in a dentist's clinic although I am reliably informed some do.

The owner of one of these dogs, a woman of ample proportions, kept telling me that she could collect her dog herself, but only at home. I didn't have the time to pack all my equipment up, then heft it to her place, which was at Ravensdown in Dunedin (I was in Helensburgh, up the hill), set up again and do the collection. So I gave her the collecting gear, a test tube and a plastic collection cone.

'It is really important to keep it at about body temperature,' I lectured her. 'How will you do that?'

She just looked at me mysteriously 'No problem, Pete. Leave it to me.'

An hour later she was back at Helensburgh. I had collected another dog in her absence, and had just finished measuring the sample, centrifuging it to separate the seminal fluid from the spermatozoa, adding the required volume of extender and putting it in the chiller. I was interested. How had she kept the sample from her beloved small dog warm? With a triumphant flourish she reached into her cleavage, and with a slight twanging of elastic, produced the sample, safely enclosed in the screw-top vial. I checked it under the microscope. It was perfect and I successfully froze it. I can almost guarantee that the designers of brassieres hadn't ever thought that their product might be used for that purpose.

The last episode I shall recount on this subject, and there are many there is no space for, concerns the lady on the aeroplane.

Travel can be a wearying and lonely business, and as most will know, there is nothing glamorous about long international flights. They are tedious and exhausting, and it's always a moment of interest when you find your seat and discover who your travelling companion is. (I was once propositioned by a much older French Canadian woman on a short flight from Toronto to Cleveland and was fortunate to be able to escape to the backwoods of Ohio in a taxi, alone.)

On a trip from Washington to London, I found myself seated beside a particularly attractive woman in a business suit. I felt that there would at least be some intellectual company here, and began to talk with her soon after take-off. She was, I think, a lawyer, travelling to London on business, and had her laptop, something pretty rare in the 1990s to a travelling New Zealander. When she found out I was a vet, she was interested and wanted to know what I was doing. I was a fellow professional. It was the first of the four or five major international trips I did with dog reproduction, and I hadn't thought this through very well.

'I collect and freeze dog semen,' I said blithely.

With a shocked look, she turned firmly away from me, and for the next 10 hours, I read my book and dozed. At Heathrow, she gathered her gear and pushed rapidly out of the aeroplane without so much as a glance at me. A city girl, I think.

But I still have friends in the several hundred dogs who I successfully collected. Most of them never forgot me, and although I can't claim to receive Christmas cards from many, it was satisfying to know that one was loved by one's patients. Quite unlike dentists, you know.

LARGE ANIMAL PRACTICE — PA

As veterinarians, especially those working with production animals, we are involved with health rather than disease. While it is important to understand the symptoms and effects of different diseases and how to treat them if practical or economically viable to do so, prevention is far more important. This can, for some diseases, involve a vaccination programme but generally most production-limiting problems in livestock are the result of inadequate feeding or feeding the wrong stuff. As in human health, 'we are what we eat'. Much of our production animal work therefore revolves around working with farmers to identify what and when nutritional factors are limiting flock or herd performance. Sometimes mineral or trace element deficiencies are involved, but more often than not it is the quality or quantity of the pasture or crop or supplement they are being fed that is limiting production. While intestinal parasites are frequently blamed for poor flock and herd performances, it can be argued that parasitism is more a reflection of inadequate management, such as inappropriate feeding, than the actual cause of poor performance. Controlling parasites using anthelmintics is the biggest single animal health cost on most sheep and beef farms.

For any herd or flock, overall performance is determined by the growth rate of young stock and the productive (wool, milk, meat) and reproductive performance of adults. Optimising lambing and calving percentages, lamb and calf weaning weights, weights of finishing stock, and milk and wool production, is therefore critical to production animal performance and for farms to remain viable. Unfortunately, by the end of the first decade of the twenty-first century, sheep-farming profitability was the lowest it has been since the middle of the twentieth century. While the best way to improve profitability is to invest in those areas that are going to improve productivity, such as fertiliser, fencing, and animal health, it is very difficult for farmers to be enthusiastic about doing this when the price they receive for the product they produce is so low that it is actually below the cost of production.

However, there is light at the end of the tunnel and very recently there has been an improvement in international commodity prices. The return for wool and meat has improved to the point that, for the first time in a very long time, we are seeing sheep and beef farmers showing some enthusiasm and optimism for the future. It is much more fun working with happy farmers.

Unfortunately this prolonged period of poor sheep farm profitability has meant many vets have found sheep and beef practice financially unrewarding as well and have left this sector of the industry. Some have become dairy vets, while others have turned their attention to other areas of their practice and concentrated on horses or deer or alpacas or small animals. Hopefully with the improved outlook for sheep and beef farming, more young vets will be encouraged to work in this area and farmers will be more enthusiastic about investing in animal health and the performance of their livestock.

With very few exceptions, to remain viable most production animal veterinary practices have had to rely on the sale of over the counter (OTC) products. But because of competition from stock firms and other traders, the margins for OTC products are small, and to compensate for falling returns from such products, fees have had to increase. As vets we prefer this arrangement and would be very happy not to have to rely on OTC sales to survive. Surviving off fees alone would be great but realistically it is impossible for most practices. One study showed that even the very busiest dairy practices covering many farms, all in close proximity to the clinic, could not charge out more than an average of four hours per vet per day. In extensive sheep and beef practices, it is far less. The cost of travel and the fee to examine and treat an individual animal is far higher than the value of the actual animal, so unless it is a valuable animal such as a horse or bull we don't end up doing a great deal of 'treating' in a sheep and beef practice. Rural vets are often perceived by farmers as being an expense they would prefer not to have to have.

Farmers are price takers. They have little say in what they are paid for their product, and so the only way many feel they can improve their bank balance is to cut costs. This approach is sometimes encouraged by their accountant or banker. In reality the best way to improve their profitability is to increase production, and that may involve investing more, rather than less, in the real drivers of farm profitability, such as fertiliser, fencing and animal health. Tightening the belt invariably leads to a downward spiral and a farm's failure to be profitable cannot always be blamed on the rising dollar, increasing farm running costs and falling returns for one or other commodity.

As we age, the enthusiasm for pregnancy testing hundreds of cows at the back of beyond under sometimes unpleasant conditions or doing an emergency calving in the middle of a paddock in a cold southerly wears thin. Too many 'older' vets who have acquired a huge amount of local knowledge over a whole life spent in a certain locality find that they have to get out. Most cannot suddenly adapt to being a small animal practitioner. However, there may be a nine to five job at the local works or drug company with far better remuneration, so they leave the industry. That knowledge acquired over many years working with farmers is lost. This is a huge loss to the rural industry.

For this reason some of us who enjoy the advisory side of the work, and who start to find the hands-on practical stuff getting a little hard on an ageing body, tend to become 'consultants'. Improving farm productivity and profitability by becoming involved in all aspects of farm management is where many of us feel we have an important role to play. We can still remain a useful member of a veterinary team without being burdened by what can be stressful after-hours and weekend duties. A minority of rural sheep and beef vets do actually make a reasonable income out of doing solely advisory work. Most are, however, part of a bigger veterinary team supplying a full veterinary service to the local farmers.

Whatever the drawbacks of large animal practice, I wouldn't have swapped it for any job in the world. It has at times been very demanding but has always been interesting. It has involved a huge range of intriguing and complex production and performance problems which have had to be sorted out. However, for me to pursue my passion for sheep and beef work has required the acceptance and goodwill of initially PJ, and in later years Stuart Burrough and Mark Wiseman. The acceptance that I would not be the main income earner, that I would be spending much of my time under less pressure than them in the countryside, and with people I loved, that I could incorporate my hobby of flying into the job, and that I could continue to operate in later years without the stress of after-hours and weekend work has been a privilege for which I will always be grateful.

ALL AT SEA — PJ

As I think I've mentioned elsewhere, I've always loved sailing. My father had various sailing dinghies when I was very small and even had a World War II life raft with a little aluminium mast and square sail which we played in at Blueskin Bay, north of Dunedin, where the family had a crib. (That's far south talk for a bach and comes from the Scottish people who first came there in the 1840s.)

So I learnt to sail as a boy and then did some more at Te Anau as a teenager. Later with a family of my own, I decided that a keeler in the Marlborough Sounds, one of the world's great temperate zone sheltered waterways, would be a good substitute for our bach in the Nelson Lakes.

So we bought a Cavalier 32, a solid 1970s design, which had been a revelation in its day and which was forgiving towards learner sailors, as we were. People had even sailed round the globe in them.

After a while I could sail it by myself and one weekend when Ally had taken the children to see her family in Canterbury, I decided it was time I went out by myself on *Fulani*.

I cast off and motored her out of the berth at the Waikawa Marina, the ageing Volvo diesel growling away. Once out in the bay, I used the autohelm to hold course while I got the mainsail up. Then the furling headsail, and we were away and sailing. The brilliance of that feeling will not be lost on those who sail. Wonderful, exhilarating, harvesting the winds to take you travelling in beautiful surroundings and to test your skills. I always relax and forget all about the everyday worries when there's a sail up.

I tacked down to the Bay of Many Coves, dropped sail and motored into the little bay where the yacht club mooring was. It wasn't there — it must have broken or more likely a clumsy power boat skipper had run over it. But there was another mooring nearby, a white buoy with Searay Charters on one side. There was no one around so I picked up the buoy, then fastened the line to *Fulani*'s bow, and congratulated myself. I went below, boiled the kettle and read my book, hoping no charter boat would turn up. But about 5.30, near dusk, a putt-putting got me poking my head through the companionway and there was a slightly larger yacht, a Lotus 10.6, approaching. Oh hell.

'Hello', I called, 'I'm on your mooring, I'll get off.' A friendly face at the helm was smiling.

'Don't worry, we can raft up and share it.'

I knew that face, another vet. And sure enough, Alex McDougall, the head vet of the Meat Division of the Ministry of Agriculture, and in an elevated position in veterinary ranks, was with his wife in the boat, which they owned and leased back to the charter company. They were convivial and welcoming, and the upshot was that we shared a meal and a couple of bottles of red. During the pleasant evening I said we had a scallop dredge on board and we could go for a drag in the bay tomorrow, which we did.

I'd never used it before, but my brother Denis had left it with me only recently, with 300 feet of braided line. So next morning Alex and I experimented with two or three drags across the Bay of Many Coves, caught 30 or 40 keeping sized scallops, and went back to his boat for lunch.

'I'm meeting James Heremaia tonight,' said Alan. 'He's got a share in this boat and we're off to the Pelorus Sound for a week's cruising.'

James Heremaia at the time was an even more senior public servant, the Chief Veterinary Officer no less, more or less the gaffer.

'Then you'll need a scallop dredge. Take mine and you can drop it back on my boat when you come back.'

The offer was accepted and I left the dredge with Alex. The next day at work, I mentioned to Pete Anderson about meeting Alex, the scallop dredge, James Heremaia, etc.

Pete looked at me strangely. 'The scallop season is closed,' he said. 'It closed at the end of February.'

So two of the most senior officials in the then New Zealand Ministry of Agriculture and Fisheries were off somewhere in the Pelorus Sound, fishing for scallops out of season.

I thought about it briefly.

'No one will notice them,' I thought. 'It's pretty unpopulated round there.'

I considered, momentarily, calling them on the VHF radio on Channel 65, but it was a bit new to me and I couldn't remember the boat's name to call. It'll be all right.

Ten days later I was at work and the phone rang. 'Alex McDougall.'

'Oh, gidday, Alex, how's things?' I said nervously.

'You might have bloody told me it was out of season,' he growled. 'We got nicked.'

A diligent resident had seen them dragging for scallops and had rung the Ministry of Ag and Fish. When they returned to Picton to the charter company berth, two uniformed MAF officers were waiting on the wharf.

The questioning was detailed, the answers given (as far as I could ascertain) were along the lines of 'experimental fishing for oysters' and it would be less than naïve to believe that an exchange of business cards took place. I am reliably informed that no prosecution was entered into. How the wheels of bureaucracy can turn in different directions. But it would have been a difficult moment for the two erstwhile gents.

Some months later, the replica of James Cook's *Endeavour* came to New Zealand. We met her at the entrance to the Sounds, by now in my newer yacht, *Ten Speed*. It was a marvellous occasion, heavy and sentimental with the drama of the historic moment, as the wonderful replica, in full sail, came into the bay to which Cook had returned five times on his three great voyages. The bush on the hills was little changed in 200 years and the Maori waka full of bare-topped paddlers alongside the copy of the great ship had me gulping back tears of emotion. As one of my friends would say, the bladder was getting close to the eyeballs.

Later, as we motored towards Picton in a huge flotilla of boats of all kinds, accompanying the brilliant replica, I realised there was a Lotus 10.6 with a familiar red stripe on the hull, right beside *Ten Speed*.

'Hello, Alex,' I called. 'Had any scallops lately?'

He tapped his mate on the shoulder and pointed accusingly towards me.

'That's him there,' I could plainly see him mouthing to his

senior colleague standing beside him in the cockpit, glass in steady hand.

I *think* they were smiling, but not very much.

Names in this story have been changed.

REFLECTIONS — PA

As we approach the end of our careers, I look back and reflect with pride on what PJ and I have achieved. Neither of us can claim any fame for publishing lots of peer-reviewed papers in leading veterinary journals — for some a measure of an individual's expertise and standing in the profession — but we have never backed down from an opportunity. We have always been prepared to take risks and give things a go when an opportunity arose. Some were successful while others were costly experiences.

We were innovative in a number of ways, and there were several reasons for this. However, probably the most significant factor was the very extensive nature of the province. We had to be realistic about what we could handle. We worked in well with our neighbouring veterinary practices and we had good clients, many of whom were close friends and who we liked to think trusted us.

As a result, along with the other local vets, it was not too difficult to implement our own deer develveting scheme well before the national one was started. Some of the national scheme was based on what we had working in Marlborough.

Another programme we implemented early on was to control *Brucella ovis*, which was rampant throughout the country in the 1960s and 1970s. This is a venereal disease of sheep and while it does cause the odd abortion, its main effect is to cause infertility in rams. We implemented our own control scheme before a national accreditation scheme began. Later with the national scheme in place, and with the excellent cooperation of our sheep farming clients, we soon had very good control of the disease, and have maintained that in our own client flocks for at least the last 20 years.

Most sheep and beef farmers spend their lives trying to improve the performance of their flocks and herds. In the case of commercial farmers, they do this by improving feeding management and by buying the best bulls and rams from stud farmers who have animals similar to the ones they aspire to have. Stud breeders also improve the genetics of their studs by buying top sires from other studs. They have also introduced new genetics by using artificial insemination or AI. This has been extremely important in the dairy and beef industries for many years.

Artificial insemination using frozen or fresh semen is a relatively simple process in the cow. However, in the sheep, introducing new genetics using artificial insemination and frozen semen is a more complex process and requires skill with a laparoscope. In the early 1980s artificial insemination of sheep was becoming popular and some of the local farmers, especially stud merino farmers, wanted to be able to inseminate their top ewes using frozen semen, mainly from Australia.

Few people had the expertise to do this, so PJ went to Australia to learn the technique for both collecting and freezing semen and for inseminating ewes. He became an expert in this field and then carried on to develop this expertise in the canine world.

When angora and cashmere goats became fashionable, there was a high demand for purebred animals. This stimulated a demand for embryo transfer. With artificial insemination the genetics of a top male could be used over literally thousands of females, but top females could only contribute to one or two offspring. However, with embryo transfer (ET) the female would be induced to shed many eggs. Hence with a good 'flush', 20 to 30 embryos or fertilised eggs might be able to be collected from a top female. We were early on the scene to learn the technique and did a lot of early ET work in goats. Later we used our skills doing embryo transfers in hinds.

We were one of the earliest sheep and beef practices to introduce a so-called planned animal health and production scheme when, for the first time, vets started looking at sheep flock and beef herd performances, and put in place animal health programmes to prevent problems. Following on from that, and in conjunction with a local sheep pregnancy scanner, Jeff Sewell, we did ground-breaking analysis of scanning and lamb survival data from sheep flocks.

We were also involved in quite a bit of on-farm research, both our own and for drug companies. For companies it involved drench, dip and vaccine trials. One important vaccine trial was with Schering-Plough's Campylovexin vaccine when, for the first time, the significance of the *Campylobacter* bacteria in causing lamb loss, and not just abortions, was illustrated. We have also spent a good deal of time and energy trying to determine the importance of vitamin E deficiency in New Zealand's pasture-fed free-range animals.

I have, over the years, also wasted time. When certain species became popular I have upskilled on them. At different times rabbits, possums and fitches or ferrets were farmed in the area for their fur. I studied them up and became relatively knowledgeable on all of them. I even went to Tasmania and studied salmon farming. For the first three it was a waste of time because the ventures were unprofitable and within a relatively short time all the farms folded. With the possum venture, it wasn't helped by an unfortunate breakout, many of the escapees waiting on the railway line close by for the next train, with rather tragic results. In the case of salmon my expertise did not seem to be required. At the time there were two major competing companies in the Marlborough Sounds and I suspect they might have felt threatened by an independent. I drew the line, however, when ostriches and emus became fashionable. Wisely I felt it was time for someone else to become the local expert. I would stick with sheep and beef cattle.

I have had the pleasure of working with some excellent large animal vets in our practice. Rob Ander worked alongside me for a number of years. Rob was a real worker and very capable and was only really happy if he was busy. Always with a cheery smile and immensely popular with the clients, he was a pleasure to work with. A very capable Scotsman, John Howie, joined the practice for a couple of years. His accent and sense of humour kept us and the clients amused for much of the time. John and I agreed to disagree on what was a more difficult job — being a sheep vet or a dairy vet. For the last couple of years, Mary Bowron has been part of the team and has had to fill some pretty big shoes after Rob left. However, she has tackled the job with enthusiasm, is a pleasure to have on the team, and has been quickly accepted by the local farmers.

In 1998 Pete and I joined forces with Stuart Burrough and built a new clinic. We lost our Pete and Pete's Pussy Parlour tag and became The Vet Centre (Malborough). We know that the practice will remain in good hands as Stuart is an excellent business man and an outstanding small animal veterinarian. It really has been a pleasure being in practice with this gentle compassionate man. He is one of the country's leading clinicians and has also been the president of the Australian College of Veterinary Scientists, members of which are Australian and New Zealand vets who have passed specialist postgraduate examinations. Stuart is these days an examiner for the college.

Not all of our work life has been that happy and easy. At the end of his veterinary career PJ and Ally lost their beautiful talented engineer daughter Jane, in the French Alps on a climbing trip. Pete has written about this so there is no need for me to elaborate. However, it is only when a tragedy like this happens to people close to you that you realise the impact it has on people's lives. They, along with their two other children, Tom and Pip, have shown huge courage in coping with this tragedy. My admiration for the manner in which they have pulled themselves out of this horrific period in their lives is endless. Coping no doubt has been greatly helped and made possible by the support and affection shown by the many friends they have built up over the years in Marlborough.

This support from family, clients and friends has also been a significant factor in helping me cope with cancer. In late 2005 I was diagnosed with multiple myeloma, a bone marrow cancer. I was not particularly surprised, because I had had some warnings. The hardest part at the beginning was telling Caroline and George what I had and that the prognosis was not really that good. My best chance was a bone marrow or stem cell transplant. Very fortunately both my brothers were good matches and after a fairly arduous preparation I underwent both an autograft using my own stem cells, and then a few weeks later, an allograft with my younger brother Jeremy's stem cells. It was an emotional moment lying in hospital after a day of being nuked with chemotherapy and total body radiation, seeing both my brothers at the end of the bed and watching Jeremy's life-saving stem cells slowly being infused into me.

I have huge respect and gratitude for the bone marrow transplant team at Christchurch Hospital. It can't be an easy job dealing with patients who often, if not close to death, are certainly feeling like it. To be treated at all times by a warm, kindly, understanding and compassionate nurse or doctor was so important when it could have been so easy for them to express even the slightest displeasure at the mess you might have just made.

While I wouldn't wish having to deal with cancer on anyone, I believe at the end of the day after facing it, surviving the treatment and recovering, I am a better person for it. I value friendships more and have a far greater respect for all those, including my family, who have been an influence on my life. I also don't tend to 'sweat the small stuff' quite so much.

These stories could have been very different or may never have happened if it wasn't for Chick and Ally.

In my case, I might have never graduated with my veterinary degree if Chick had not put some stability into my student days. My academic performance before she came along had been mediocre to say the least.

Later, during PJ and my early days in business, she and Ally worked in their own careers, as well as for us, and almost single-handedly raised our children.

I will also be forever indebted to Chick for the manner in which she has managed everything and nursed me through the times I have been recuperating from various injuries, sickness and cancer.

And for the future — who knows what lies ahead? I don't really ever want to fully retire. With a bit of luck, I will carry on for a few more years yet doing what I love doing with the wonderful people with whom I have been so privileged to spend a lifetime.

DARKNESS AND LIGHT — PJ

This book was to have been published four years earlier, in 2007.

When Pete A became ill in 2005, and was in the process of a stem cell transplant, a fearsome and debilitating affair, he became pretty moribund. We had talked about writing a book together for years, and we had a list of topics more or less drawn up. In an attempt to find something positive for him, I suggested he start the writing we'd always planned.

He did, and the result was brilliant. Before long he had half a dozen very funny and well-written stories finished. That inspired me to get cracking too, and before long we were in touch with the Dunedin publishing house, Longacre Press, who had encouraged me to write more after I had co-authored a book on training working dogs.

The result was that we had a contract sitting on my desk in July 2007, three months after I had retired from practice.

Then the sky fell in.

Our beloved and brilliant daughter, Jane, died in the mountains in France. She was 26.

Only parents who have experienced the loss of a child can truly understand the utter desolation that follows. The pain is indescribable, and it is impossible to function fully and normally for a long time afterwards. I don't think it ever goes away.

Jane was an extraordinary young woman: dux of her school, a sportswoman, and an ebullient character with a large circle of friends. She had always had a feeling that she wasn't as clever as her siblings (not so) and had spent the second half of her life proving that she could do everything.

An engineer with first-class honours from Canterbury University, she had gone to Grenoble in 2003 to do a masterate, a one-year concentrated course. Fatefully, she graduated first in the class, which earned her a French government scholarship to stay on and complete a doctorate, another three years.

She contacted us most days, certainly every week, by email, phone, text, and even real letters. She shared her hopes and fears, her adventures and her doubts. She was our friend as much as our daughter. She returned home three times in the four years in France; we visited her on three occasions.

She sang in a semi-professional ensemble, rock climbed, tramped in the Pyrenees, cycled to work every day. She fell in love with a fellow engineer, Yorkshireman Mark Emerson, an alpine climber.

With two other young friends they began to climb peaks in the Alps, and in the mountain ranges which surround Grenoble. They did ice climbing and safety courses. Their goal was to climb Mont Blanc, Europe's largest peak, and visible from the hills above Grenoble on a clear day.

On 23 July 2007, Jane, Mark, a Chilean woman Mariana

Huerta, and a French woman Morgane Clément were caught at 4000 metres by a sudden and devastating summer storm on the Dome de Goûter, a shoulder of Mont Blanc, on the fourth and final day of their climb. Over the following 12 hours, battered by the storm, with temperatures of -30°C, the four friends succumbed to hypothermia and exhaustion. They were half an hour from shelter. It was my sixtieth birthday.

Jane was four months from graduating with her doctorate. The thesis was mostly written, the field work complete.

Three months later I returned to Grenoble with my much-loved brother-in-law to scatter some of their ashes, with 50 of their friends and colleagues, on La Dent de Crolles, a peak in the Chartreuse mountains above Grenoble. A year later, Ally and I went back to Grenoble for Jane's soutenance, or defence of her doctorate thesis. A group of eminent geotechnical experts from around the world heard Pierre Foray, Jane's professor and mentor, deliver her findings. The doctorate was duly awarded *In Memoriam*, scant comfort for Jane's family, but recognition of her contribution to science. Her specialty (as was Mark's) was liquefaction of sedimentary soils in earthquakes. They had both secured jobs in Canterbury. It is bitter irony that the 2010 and 2011 earthquakes there would have given her the opportunity to play a vital role in the rebuilding of Christchurch.

In the months that followed, our friends and extended families kept us alive, and a new property we had moved into only three weeks before their accident kept us busy. The sudden halting of the omnipresent communications from Jane was shocking, and very difficult to believe. I found myself checking my mail every day, just in case. I wept in the shower every morning, and in many other places and times. It seemed so outrageous.

We did what we could to keep Jane's memory alive. We

dedicated a new drama block at Marlborough Girls' College to her, with a large illustrated plate on a wall. We put a beautiful macrocarpa seat, Jane's Seat, on top of the Wither Hills behind Blenheim. And we scattered the remainder of hers and Mark's ashes on the St Arnaud range in the Nelson Lakes, a place where Jane and Mark had spent a lot of time together. Point 1787, above Parachute Rocks, will always be known to us as Jane's Peak.

The first year after the accident is a blur of horror, misery, disbelief and above all, darkness. It was hard to feel good about anything. I look back to that time and see just darkness. I served a three-year term on the Veterinary Council of New Zealand, but never came to terms with the stultifying bureaucracy of Wellington, even if the people in the council were nice.

The next year there was a by-election for the Marlborough District Council, one of New Zealand's five unitary authorities, after a resignation. My friend Ron Crosby urged me to stand, but I wasn't initially interested. He persisted, and at the eleventh hour I put my nomination in. It was one of the scariest things I've ever done, putting myself up to be judged by my community, but I was lucky enough to be elected, and then re-elected in 2010. It's been a good and positive experience; the chance to put something back into a community that's been very good to me and my family gives me a lot of pleasure. Now in 2011 in my second term, there are plenty of challenges. As chair of the environment committee I have some major long-term responsibilities for Marlborough's future.

This was the first ray of light, following the darkness.

The second, and even brighter, was the birth of our first grandchild in November 2010. Abbi Jane Jerram was produced by our lovely Irish daughter-in-law Dinah and our son Tom. Already she makes me feel more positive, a growing continuation of life.

Gradually, and with growing confidence, I can feel myself looking at the good things. I feel strongly the need to leave our world as good as we found it, in sound environmental and economic health, but in that order, for future generations. I see great hope for our children as they go forward in life, despite the loss of their sister. Pippa, Jane's sister and best friend, wrote and sang a hauntingly beautiful song at the memorial service in Blenheim, and gradually music, always a major part of our lives, is returning.

I also see Pete A battling with his condition. He's tremendous, brave, understanding of himself and positive. He refuses to let it stop him from enjoying life. His wife Chick and their adult children, Caroline and George, are our dear friends for life.

We've had a wonderful 32 years together, and I'm sure we've got a few more yet. It was a good career, with many rewarding and many challenging moments. For three years after Jane's death, I was unable to write, or to even think about it. Now, I can feel the creative juices flowing again, and I've really enjoyed putting our stories together.

I hope you've enjoyed them as much as we enjoyed being part of them.